ignatieff's world

iggy goes to ottawa

updated

denis smith

JAMES LORIMER & COMPANY LTD., PUBLISHERS
TORONTO

Copyright © 2009 by Denis Smith

All rights reserved. No part of this book may be reproduced or transmitted in any form or by any means, electronic or mechanical, including photocopying, or by any information storage or retrieval system, without permission in writing from the publisher.

James Lorimer & Company Ltd. acknowledges the support of the Ontario Arts Council. We acknowledge the support of the Government of Canada through the Book Publishing Industry Development Program (BPIDP) for our publishing activities. We acknowledge the support of the Canada Council for the Arts for our publishing program.We acknowledge the support of the Government of Ontario through the Ontario Media Development Corporation's Ontario Book Initiative.

Cover design: Meghan Collins

Library and Archives Canada Cataloguing in Publication

Smith, Denis, 1932-
    Ignatieff's world updated : Iggy goes to Ottawa / Denis Smith.

ISBN 978-1-55277-406-9

    1. Ignatieff, Michael—Political and social views.
2. Canada—Politics and government—2006-.
3. Politicians—Canada—Biography. I. Title.

FC641.I35S65 2009   971.07'3092   C2009-900986-2

James Lorimer & Company Ltd., Publishers
317 Adelaide Street West, Suite 1002
Toronto, Ontario, M5V 1P9
www.lorimer.ca

Printed and bound in Canada.

contents

ACKNOWLEDGEMENTS

I am grateful, once again, to Eric Bergbusch, Stephen Clarkson, and Mel Watkins for their comments on the additions to the manuscript of this new edition; to my agent Bella Pomer; to Jim Lorimer and his staff for their care and swiftness in managing a fast publication schedule; and to Dawn for her unfailing advice and support.

PREFACE

The first edition of this book was published in 2006, during Michael Ignatieff's first campaign for the leadership of the Liberal Party of Canada. I concluded then that he was not the right person to lead the party. The leadership convention eventually shared that view. Now, less than three years and one general election later, the Liberal Party has returned to Parliament with Michael Ignatieff as its "interim" leader: installed, anointed, crowned (but not yet elected), the outcome of an extraordinary outburst of political theatre played over two weeks late in 2008 before a startled national audience. He will almost certainly be confirmed by unanimous vote of the delegates at the party's national convention in Vancouver in May 2009.

In December 2006, after his fourth ballot defeat at the Montreal convention, it was clear that Michael Ignatieff's political story would not end with its opening chapter. He had returned to Canada to seek the leadership of the Liberal Party, and no one doubted that he would seek it again. His supporters and advocates in the party remained on standby while he established his record as an MP. But his sudden accession to the leadership in 2008 came as a surprise—both to the party and to the country.

Who is this man who glowers and beams so imperiously at us from beneath his thick, black eyebrows? What is his background? What does he believe? Where does he fit on the political spectrum? How did he eliminate his leadership rivals without a public contest? What kind of alternative does he offer to the Conservative Party of Stephen Harper?

The opening section of this book, Cosmopolitan, contains the text of the first edition published in September 2006. In it I review and assess Michael Ignatieff's views on international policy as expressed in his writings and speeches prior to his first leadership contest. These controversial views are still largely unknown to Canadian voters. They would be of no general significance to Canadians if he had continued his academic and literary career in Canada or abroad. But now that he seeks to lead the country, they are relevant as guides to his vision of the world, his character, and his judgement.

The second part of the book, Tough Guy, contains an account of his recent career in Canadian politics, from the leadership campaign of 2006 to his role as deputy leader of the Liberal Party in the House of Commons, to the election campaign of 2008, to the extraordinary events that thrust him unexpectedly into the leadership, to the budget vote of February 2009. This is not narrative history, but a focused study of Ignatieff's role in the politics of those years. How much has he learned as a practising politician? How have his views changed? Is he, in any essential ways, a different man than he was when he entered active politics in the autumn of 2005? What does the record reveal about how he might lead the country as prime minister? In the spring of 2009 the story remains unfinished.

*   *   *

Michael Ignatieff is a Canadian who made his career as a public intellectual in Great Britain and the United States. He gained a notable reputation abroad as the author of more than a dozen works of political commentary, biography, and fiction, and as a prolific contributor to the *New York Review of Books*, the *New York Times*, the *New Yorker*, the *New Republic*, the *Guardian*, the *Observer*, the CBC, the BBC, and the British monthly *Prospect*. Not surprisingly, he was better known in Britain and the United States than in Canada—until he returned to Canada as a Liberal candidate in the 2006 federal election. When he won his parliamentary seat and then, weeks later, announced his candidacy for the Liberal leadership, his face, his voice, and his articulate views were suddenly thrust upon the nation. His advocates, then as now, saw him as a rescuer who would breathe new life into the party, restore its confidence, and lead it back to power where it belongs. But his critics have good reasons for their doubts.

The pattern of Ignatieff's thought on international politics showed a steady evolution from the mid-1980s until 2005. When he entered public discussion in Great Britain at the end of the Cold War, he stepped into a comfortable Canadian tradition, that of the liberal internationalist. As the fragile stability of the Cold War disappeared and rigidity collapsed into chaos in the old Soviet empire, central Europe, and the Middle East, Ignatieff came to describe himself as an optimistic "humanitarian interventionist," promoting the use of international rules and institutions to encourage the restoration of civil order and the spread of democracy. In Northern Ireland, Afghanistan, Iraq, Bosnia, Croatia, Serbia, Kosovo, Rwanda, and South Africa, he observed a series of deadly political struggles and offered suggestions for recovery and treatment of the wounds.

Much of his attention in the 1990s was devoted to the violent disintegration of the Federal Republic of Yugoslavia. As the horrors continued there, Ignatieff became an advocate of Western military intervention in the southern Yugoslav province of Kosovo, where the majority population of Albanian Muslims suffered growing repression at the hands of the Serbian-dominated central government. In March 1999, the North Atlantic Treaty Organization (NATO), acting under American leadership, attacked Serbia from the air in an effort to dislodge the Serbian police and military from the province. Throughout this campaign, Ignatieff defended the attack, despite the vast exodus of Kosovo Albanians fleeing across international borders to emergency refugee camps in Macedonia and Albania, and despite a devastating seventy-eight-day NATO bombing campaign against Serbia. Afterwards, he wondered aloud whether that televised "virtual war" of aerial bombardment—conducted safely from high altitude and without casualties in the offensive alliance—might encourage further destructive acts by the United States and its allies in other places. His musings were prophetic.

During the Kosovo War, many progressives in Britain, the United States, and Canada seemed to share Ignatieff's views. That was true even though there were widespread and troubling doubts about the morality of the NATO attack on Serbia—an aggression undertaken without the authority of the UN Security Council—which Ignatieff continued to defend. But soon afterwards, he broke away from the mainstream of liberal international opinion.

In 2001, one terrible day dominated our minds. The suicide attacks by Al Qaeda on targets in New York and

Washington were brutally shocking and unsettling—because of their scale, their location, their appalling simplicity, and their inhumanity. For everyone in the West, absorbing the fact of these attacks—and making any sense of them—took months. In the aftermath of the terrorist attacks in the United States this prominent advocate of human rights (who was by then director of the Carr Center for Human Rights Policy at Harvard University) seemed to lose his moral equilibrium. Ignatieff adopted the tone and language used by President George W. Bush as he launched a worldwide "war on terrorism." The prominent Canadian observer became an apologist for assertive American dominance in the world (which he had described in 2003 as "Empire Lite"); he supported the United States and Britain as they prepared to invade Iraq in defiance of the UN Security Council and most of America's allies; he defended emergency restrictions on civil liberties and large-scale internments in Afghanistan and the United States; and he argued for the use of "coercive interrogation" against terror suspects. For four years after the initial American occupation of Iraq in 2003, Ignatieff continued to defend the invasion (if not its destructive aftermath) on the grounds that a cruel dictator had been deposed and the eventual recovery of order remained a possibility. Only in 2007 did he offer a convoluted admission of error in the pages of the *New York Times Magazine*.

Ignatieff's justifications for his views on the American empire, the "war on terror," "nation-building," the Iraq War, and the treatment of terror suspects were laid out in his book *The Lesser Evil* (2004). In making his case for emergency measures, he offered dubious arguments, ignored historical context, and overcomplicated the moral landscape.

Ignatieff's general commitment to human rights was obscured, or even lost, as he hardened himself against the cruel world and asked his readers to join him in defence of American power. The issues he dealt with in that book and elsewhere involve tough moral questions about human life and death, civil rights and political freedom, state sovereignty, and the consequences of American leadership. All these dilemmas now face him as leader of the Liberal Party of Canada.

When he first campaigned for leadership of the party in 2006, Ignatieff was a freshman MP sitting on the opposition benches. Later, speaking at a fund-raiser, he mused about the outcome of the 2006 general election and its effect on his fortunes in the party:

> You'll remember January 23, 2006. I thought we'd win. Instead, we lost. I thought Mr. Martin would stay on as leader. He resigned the night of the election. So I hadn't been an MP for five minutes before the press was treating me as the front-runner for the leadership.
>
> And so it went till the Convention in Montreal: front-runner all the way to the fourth ballot and a second place finish to Stéphane Dion.

The rookie MP, newly returned to Canada after a twenty-year absence, with thoughts of an eventual contest to succeed Paul Martin, was thrust prematurely into that campaign. The convention delivered the prize to Stéphane Dion; as consolation Ignatieff was appointed deputy leader of the party in the House of Commons.

Under Dion, the Liberals at first predicted a short term in opposition, a smartly-timed defeat of Stephen Harper's minority government, an election victory, and a comforting return to power. But those dreams were confounded. Stéphane Dion performed awkwardly and incoherently in the House of Commons, and was cruelly mocked in Conservative advertising campaigns. The Harper government maintained its lead in the opinion polls through 2007 and 2008, though without ever achieving firm majority support. The Liberal Party made no gains in popularity and failed to reorganize or pay off the debts of its 2006 leadership candidates. It was in no condition to conduct an effective national election campaign. By the spring of 2008, the hapless new leader was avoiding an election by repeatedly directing his MPs to absent themselves *en masse* from confidence votes in the House. The party seemed cowardly and directionless. As deputy leader, Michael Ignatieff stood at Stéphane Dion's left shoulder: a prospective heir who outshone the leader in the House while always professing loyalty to the incumbent.

Prime Minister Stephen Harper dominated the House of Commons by default. During the summer of 2008, as the Liberal caucus stiffened its spine and prepared to defeat the government when Parliament reconvened, Harper chose his own moment to go to the people. The House, he declared, had become "dysfunctional." Ignoring his own fixed election law, he dissolved Parliament for a mid-October election.[1] This way he avoided the "Obama effect" by getting the Canadian election out of the way before the American vote three weeks later; and he also hoped to get a majority government in place before the onset of a deepening recession.

The Canadian public endured the distasteful election

campaign of 2008 mostly by ignoring it. Potential Liberal supporters stayed away from the polls in the thousands, and the party lost twenty of its parliamentary seats. Stephen Harper returned the largest bloc of MPs, but deprived his own party of a majority by his mean-spirited cuts to the arts budget, a crude campaign against youth crime, and his denial of any need for economic stimulus as the country tumbled rapidly into economic decline. The Bloc Québécois held its own, and Jack Layton's NDP made modest gains.

Stéphane Dion was the first victim of this futile election. He quickly offered his resignation as party leader. But he also gave notice that he would stay on until the party chose a successor in May 2009. The Liberal Party—demoralized and unsettled by its electoral failure—did nothing to counter the imprudent decision of its discredited leader to lead the party through six crucial months in the House of Commons in the midst of a campaign to replace him. Within weeks, Michael Ignatieff, Bob Rae, and Dominic LeBlanc announced their candidacies for the leadership.

For Harper, the prospect of the new Parliament seemed an unanticipated gift: despite his minority, he would face a weak and distracted opposition. Instead of taking advantage he made himself victim of his own mysterious demons.

On November 27, the minister of finance delivered a financial update that defied the evidence by predicting a budgetary surplus, and insulted both opposition and public in a display of petty spitefulness. Within days, Canada's politicians had turned a series of somersaults. The combined opposition gave notice of its intention to defeat the government and install the lame duck Stéphane Dion as a coalition prime minister; Harper indicted his opponents as usurpers of power and obtained a parliamentary suspension from the Governor-General to avoid that defeat; and the Liberal Party (either concussed or awakened from concussion by the somersaults) threw over its normal constitutional procedures to replace Stéphane Dion with Michael Ignatieff as leader—once his two competitors, Dominic LeBlanc and Bob Rae, had gracefully withdrawn from the race. Dion quickly left town.

This gymnastic display defies close analysis, but leaves Ignatieff as the undoubted leader of the Liberal Party of Canada. The party professes itself united and confident as it has not been for two years (or two decades). For one weekend it was allied with the New Democratic Party in a coalition about to take power. It is no longer. Ignatieff speaks now of the Liberal Party as "my party." Whether it can recover its place as the country's Natural Governing Party rests in his hands. The second part of this book looks at his short political career for signs of what Canadians may expect from Michael Ignatieff in his forthcoming battles with Prime Minister Stephen Harper. How much baggage does he carry with him from his years abroad? What kind of parliamentary leader is he likely to be?[2]

Ottawa, Ontario
February 2009

part one: cosmopolitan

CHAPTER 1

Doing Something or Doing Nothing

When Michael Ignatieff entered Canadian politics in November 2005, he learned quickly that old words could return to haunt him. As he parachuted into the Ontario constituency of Etobicoke-Lakeshore for nomination as a Liberal Party candidate in the 2006 federal general election, the first reaction came from members of the local Liberal riding executive. Myroslava Oleksiuk, secretary of the constituency association, charged that he had insulted Ukraine in his book *Blood and Belonging*, published in 1993, and would not be acceptable as a candidate to the many Polish and Ukrainian immigrants in the riding. " 'My difficulty in taking Ukraine seriously,' " she quoted Ignatieff as saying, " 'goes deeper than just my cosmopolitan suspicion of nationalists everywhere. Somewhere inside, I'm also what Ukrainians would call a Great Russian and there is just a trace of old Russian disdain for these little Russians.' "[3] If this was meant as a jest, it could also have had just a trace of self-revealing truth in it. The predominantly Ukrainian-Canadian executive committee of the local Liberal riding association resigned at the sudden prospect of his candidacy, two other candidates who attempted to file nomination papers were rejected on technical grounds, and Ignatieff received the nomination by acclamation. In his acceptance speech, he emphasized his personal and family attachments to Ukraine and to the Ukrainian-Canadian community and rejected the former executive's accusation. "Anyone who reads the entire chapter in question," he said, "rather than merely the phrases that have been cited in isolation and out of context, will quickly recognize that my sole purpose was to rebut, not assert, the odious stereotype of Ukrainians that has been wrongly and unfairly attributed to me."[4]

Ignatieff won this exchange handily. He used the politician's standard reply to critics—that he had been quoted out of context—and he was right. In the book he gives wry credit to "the tendentious fanatics … who refused to accept that Soviet power would last an eternity, got it right, and the rest of us were wrong."[5] His chapter on Ukraine is a melancholy account of a journalist's tour to the newly independent nation, still suffering the lingering reality of seventy years of Soviet oppression. The chapter is a generous concession to the reality of Ukrainian independence, but there was a still larger context which Ignatieff did not mention in his Etobicoke acceptance speech. *Blood and Belonging* placed Ukrainian nationalism within the framework of six studies of ethnic or racial nationalism, and in 1993 Ignatieff had reservations about all of them. *Blood and Belonging* marked the beginning of his decade-long inquiry into the sources of ethnic strife, the breakdown of states, and the means of bringing peace and order to their unfortunate victims.

This journey took him, by stages, from a position of skeptical respect for nations struggling for dignity within the boundaries of larger states (or freshly independent from them), to a focus on the international protection of human rights, to support for military rescue missions in Bosnia and

Kosovo, to condemnation of radical Islamic terrorism after 9/11, to full-blooded defence of America's imperial role in the world, to support for the Bush/Blair invasion of Iraq in 2003. This fascinating intellectual journey was conditioned by the terrible events of two decades following the collapse of the Soviet empire in 1989. It was a journey shared by many others as they sought a fresh footing in a confusing world. Western liberals and leftists, on the whole, at first took the same path as Ignatieff, placing new hope in co-operative action to control the forces of disorder through the UN and other international agencies.

But on September 11, 2001, the world reached an unexpected crossroads. When the new American administration of George W. Bush took office nine months earlier, it signalled its desire to set its own, unilateralist course by abandoning commitments to a range of international obligations. Nevertheless, it remained focused on domestic affairs and inactive abroad until the attacks on New York and Washington. After September 11, Bush declared that the United States would launch a worldwide "war on terror," and that the nations and peoples of the world were "either for us or against us." (The definition of a "war on terror"—how to fight it, where, for how long, against whom, at what cost—came from the American president and his advisors alone, but in Western countries the phrase became the accepted description of the hazardous situation after 9/11.) As leaders made their choices, so did others. The attacks on New York and Washington were almost universally condemned; the inevitability of an American-led war against the Afghan regime harbouring the terrorist Al Qaeda movement was fatalistically accepted; and governments prepared for further—and long-term—consequences.

In the early days after the terrorist attacks, these could only be imagined.

One of those on the liberal left who chose overriding support for the American "war on terror" was Ignatieff. It was this choice, more than any other, that brought him into conflict with former allies in the international human rights movement. The acts of those who defined this "war" would repeatedly challenge his dedication to human rights, constitutionalism, democracy, and the rule of law. How could he reconcile those acts with his beliefs? What role would he play, as a prominent writer and journalist, in guiding the public and the American administration through the minefields of post-9/11? What conclusions can be drawn about his knowledge and his judgement in facing these moral dilemmas? The file is more complex than it seemed to his Ukrainian-Canadian critics in Etobicoke-Lakeshore on the eve of his nomination. It begins with *Blood and Belonging*, but includes at least five other books and numerous newspaper and magazine articles, public lectures, and interviews covering the period from 1993 to 2006.[6]

Nationalism and Internationalism

Blood and Belonging is the offshoot of a BBC series of six films on modern nationalisms. It is not a work of history or of political analysis nor does it claim to be. It is a highly personal television essay. When the project began, Ignatieff placed little value on his own or others' national identity. He had come from a prominent family, the son of a leading member of Canada's Department of External Affairs in the department's golden age of liberal internationalism after the Second World War. His mother, Alison

Grant, was the granddaughter of George Monro Grant, Principal of Queen's University. His uncle was the philosopher George Grant. Michael, born in 1947, absorbed the ethos of External Affairs as his family moved to postings in Belgium, the United States, Yugoslavia, and Ottawa, and the ethos of Canada (or privileged slices of it) as a student at Upper Canada College and Trinity College in the University of Toronto. When he left Canada for graduate work in the United States and a career in Britain, he took the values of liberal internationalism with him. At that time, in the late sixties, there was hardly any other view of the world on offer in English-speaking Canada (beyond the glimmers of student radicalism): it reached far beyond the federal civil service and the Liberal Party into the ranks of the political opposition, business, the trade unions, the universities, and the churches. Canada's activist foreign policy of support for the new United Nations, liberalized international trade, close friendship with the United States, and membership in the Western military alliance after 1949 enjoyed wide popular consensus. In the fifties, Liberal Prime Minister Louis St. Laurent even managed to gain support for this outward-looking foreign policy from a cautious, latently isolationist Quebec.

The triumph of liberal internationalism in postwar Canada was a product of the country's wartime alliance with Britain and the United States and of American recognition that the United States would have to play a generous and creative international role if other world wars were to be avoided. Given the closeness of the postwar Anglo-American alliance, it was easy and natural for Canada to make up the third liberal partner in this triangle of common purpose. The Americans of that time, Democrats or Republicans, were mostly trustworthy believers in and promoters of the same values as Canadians. Canadians could show their distaste for the occasional Senator McCarthy or Senator Taft, but slept well at night knowing that Harry Truman, Dwight Eisenhower, and Jack Kennedy were there below the border. And in Britain too their prime ministers were all liberal internationalists (until the arrival of Margaret Thatcher in 1979). It would, indeed, have been strange—given his background and the spirit of the times—if the young Ignatieff had *not* gone abroad as a liberal internationalist. By the mid-sixties, the temper of the United States was beginning to change, as it slipped into the abyss of the Vietnam war. Yet Canada held onto its predominant liberal temper for a decade or two after that.

In fact, out of the security provided by that Canadian background, Ignatieff took a step that looked to him like stepping confidently into the world's future, beyond his friends at the University of Toronto, beyond Canada. For him, the wave of the future was not Marxism but "cosmopolitanism." He described himself as a postnational cosmopolitan, dependent on the nation in which he lived only to "provide the security and the rights we all need in order to live cosmopolitan lives" among people of diverse backgrounds. But after the collapse of the Soviet empire and the end of a stable "Soviet and American joint imperium," he saw a world plunged into bitter local rivalries where communities sought safety and protection within their own ethnic boundaries. He was shocked by the ferocity of conflicts among villagers who had lived peacefully side by side for generations. What were they doing to one another? What kind of political order could give them security once more? Ignatieff set off with his BBC crew to investigate. "The itinerary I chose," he wrote, "was personal, but hopefully not arbitrary. I chose places I had lived in, cared about, and knew enough about to believe that they could illustrate certain central themes."[7]

He travelled to Yugoslavia as it was dissolving through "ethnic cleansing" into separate republics after the death of the unifying dictator Josip Broz Tito; then to Germany, in the early stages of reunification after forty-five years of division between the communist East and democratic West; then to Ukraine, emerging painfully into independence from the former Soviet Union; then to Quebec, a cultural and linguistic nation trying to decide whether it should remain within a larger multinational state; then to the Kurdish region of northern Iraq; and finally to Northern Ireland, where Catholic and Protestant paramilitaries fought to achieve different visions of society. In these conflicts he searched for some saving pattern of common life: if not his naive cosmopolitanism—of which he was now disabused—then perhaps something labelled "post-nationalism".[8] He had decided in the face of discouraging evidence that nations do, after all, fulfill basic needs. A cosmopolitan life, he recognized, "… is the privilege of those who can take a secure nation state for granted":

> … a cosmopolitan, post-nationalist spirit will always depend, in the end, on the capacity of nation states to provide security and civility for their citizens. In that sense alone, I am a civic nationalist, someone who believes in the necessity of nations and in the duty of citizens to defend the capacity of nations to provide

> the security and rights we all need in order to
> live cosmopolitan lives ...[9]

Ignatieff leaves a slight sense here that he is engaged in a juggling game with words that fail to describe the world's complexity.

Because the book grew out of a television series, the themes he pursues in *Blood and Belonging* can only emerge in occasional editorial asides. Anecdotes, unusual personal encounters, and vivid sketches of his travels make up most of the text. His descriptions of shattered landscapes, blasted communities, and personal agonies have great power. The themes emerge as experience forces his thoughts. He learns that, in many extreme situations, ethnicity and attachment to the land are matters of life and death. He learns that inter-communal violence can explode when multinational states lose their legitimacy. He sees that, rather than being the result of ethnic hatred, violence often precipitates it. And by the end of his journeys, he begins to glimpse one possible way out of the chaos of rival nationalisms. (Or is it no more than the "postnationalism" with which he began?)

On the war lines between Serbia and Croatia, where neighbours watch each other through their gunsights, the disenchanted liberal cosmopolitan stumbles through ruined towns and laments that "late twentieth-century nationalism has delivered one part of the European continent back to the time before the nation state, to the chaos of late feudal civil war."[10] He blames Tito for never preparing for the succession in his six-nation federation, and the Yugoslav public for never giving themselves time to learn how to play peacetime politics. In effect, Ignatieff charges the Serbo-Croats with a kind of collective immaturity, but he offers little history to show whose words and decisions led them into murderous civil war. He visits the ruins after the carnage, without explaining how it occurred.[11]

But the West was watching on television. When Ignatieff asks what that audience (or their leaders) might have done to prevent the disaster, he finds an opportunity missed:

> Standing back from the disaster, one begins to see that Western failures to act in time were caused by something deeper than inattention, misinformation or misguided good intentions. The very principles behind our policies were in contradiction. In the light-headed euphoria of 1989, we announced our support for the right of national self-determination and for the territorial integrity of existing states, without realizing that the first principle contradicted the second. We insisted on the inviolability of frontiers, without being clear whether we also meant the frontiers within federal states like Yugoslavia.
>
> Most of all, we allowed guilt over our imperial pasts to lead us to evade our responsibilities to define the terms of a post-imperial peace. Post-imperial societies felt guilty about condemning the nationalism of peoples who have been kept under imperial control. When the 'captive nations'—from the Baltic to the Balkans—demanded their freedom, we did not stop to consider the consequences. After Versailles, after Yalta, the collapse of the last empire in Europe offered

us a third opportunity to define a durable peace and create a new order of nations in Europe. We could have ended the Cold War with a comprehensive territorial settlement, defining borders, guaranteeing minority-rights and adjudicating between rival claims to self-determination. So concerned were we to avoid playing the imperial policeman, so self-absorbed were we in the frantic late 1980s boom, that we allowed every local post-communist demagogue to exploit the rhetoric of self-determination and national rights to his own ends. The terrible new order of ethnically cleansed states in the former Yugoslavia is the monument to our follies, as much as it is to theirs.[12]

This sudden leap from description to prescription is rare in the book, and it is followed at once by a return to personal experience, when an elderly Serb promises the author that vengeance against the Croats will continue into the next generation.

Does the claim of an opportunity missed have any substance? Where is its context? Ignatieff was speaking of the years before and after the collapse of the Berlin wall when Mikhail Gorbachev was dismantling the Soviet state and clinging to his tattered authority, George H.W. Bush was mounting and executing a war of liberation in Kuwait, John Major was learning the ropes at Westminster, and the Western world was falling into economic recession. Did anyone actually propose a new Congress of Vienna, Versailles, or Yalta? Was this what Bush intended when he carelessly threw out the promise of a "new world order" at the conclusion of the Gulf War in 1991? There was never any chance of that: no one proposed a new Versailles Conference. Ignatieff's should-have-been seems no more than a grand rhetorical flourish. Or—interpreted at its best—it was a moral admonition to the world of nations: Look at this mess! You are responsible! You must do better next time![13]

Ignatieff comes to accept the depth of national commitments to community and land, but rejects the fantasy of ethnically pure nations purged of intruding nationalities. That dream, he sees, is both unrealistic and self-destructive. Instead, in a newly reunited Germany, with its millions of foreign workers and Germans returned from the east, he offers another hope. Germany's task, he asserts, "is not, as some liberals suppose, to pass beyond nationalism altogether and move into bland Europeanism, but instead to move from the ethnic nationalism of its past to the civic nationalism of a possible future … moving away from identification with the nation towards identification with the state, away from a citizenship based on the fiction of ethnic identity towards one based on allegiance to the values of democracy."[14] This was his goal of "civic nationalism."

In his visits to both Quebec and Ukraine, Ignatieff draws on his own family's past, reluctantly accepting that there, too, genuine nations exist but must seek new levels of tolerance where strangers can "come together to form a community of equals, based not on ethnicity but on citizenship."[15] He offers the hopeful judgement that "nationalism in Quebec has long ceased to be the nationalism of resentment. The old scores have been settled. It is now a rhetoric of self-affirmation."[16] But the chapter on

Quebec consists of a handful of interviews with young Québécois and no history. Ignatieff neglects to tell his readers that Canada, in 1992, had just passed through a divisive national referendum centred on the constitutional rights of the Quebec nation (when federal proposals for reconciliation were defeated) or that the Parti Québécois had promised to hold its own referendum on independence within the province once it had returned to power. (It did so and almost won in 1995.) These were essential missing elements. For a British television audience viewing Ignatieff's journeys, they were perhaps unnecessary, but their absence left doubts about whether he knew much about his own country.

In Kurdistan, where the UN established a protectorate after the Gulf War in 1991 to stop deadly incursions by Hussein's army and air force, Ignatieff sees the human result. "The best way to find out what a nation state means to a people, what it does to their character, is to spend time among a people who have never had one of their own."[17] He admires this brave people and warmly endorses what has occurred.

> Kurdistan is something new under the sun in international law—the first attempt by the UN to protect a minority people against the genocidal intentions of its nominal ruler. Until Kurdistan, the international community stopped short of "interventions" which challenged the territorial integrity and sovereignty of nation states. With the creation of the Kurdish enclave, it endorsed the idea that the duty of humanitarian intervention over-

rode the principle of the inviolability and integrity of sovereign states. If Kurdistan works, other nations which believe they can abuse indigenous minorities with impunity may see such enclaves hacked out of their territory. Kurdistan is all that remains of George Bush's "new world order." It remains the only place where a new balance between the right of people and the right of nations for the post-Cold War world was drawn.[18]

The chapter about Kurdistan in *Blood and Belonging* is the most emotionally charged in the book. Its descriptions are consistently eloquent:

Saddam has blocked Kurdistan's borders, and a desperately poor economy is only kept going by the ingenuity of the mule drivers who bring cooking oil and soap over the mountain passes from Iran, the Turkish trucks which thunder up this road, and … oil-smeared boys who sell smuggled petrol from jerry-cans by the road-side. The boys are barefoot and look cold in the darkness. Yet somehow the atmosphere is not of poverty and desperation, but of wonder and mystery—cheekbones and brown skin in the chiaroscuro of kerosene lamps, the bowed shapes of the tents, the flaps held back to reveal the smuggled treasures within. The boys stand by the flaps, their faces lit by the kerosene lamps, their eyes beckoning me to enter.[19]

Here, Ignatieff's personal commitment to the Kurdish people
is palpable. And here too—he is undoubtedly saying—we can see
the future. This makeshift international protectorate, guarded by
air force and army units of Great Britain and the United States,
gives liberal internationalists a glimmer of hope in an otherwise
bleak landscape. It works, and people survive in peace. Although
Iraqi Kurds tell him that they do not seek independence—nothing more than safe autonomy within Iraq—Ignatieff will not
accept their word. "Statelessness is a state of mind, and it is akin
to homelessness. This is what a nationalist understands: a people
can become completely human, completely themselves, only
when they have a place of their own."[20]

After a final visit to Northern Ireland, Ignatieff tries to
make sense of what he has seen and heard on all six of his
journeys. He admits that he cannot do so. "There are puzzles
which no theory of nationalism ... can resolve. After you
have been to the wastelands of the new world order, particularly to those fields of graves, marked by numberless wooden
crosses, you feel stunned into silence by a deficit of moral
explanation."[21] Nationalism, he says, "is a form of speech
which shouts, not so that it will be heard, but so that it will
believe itself." There are no ethnically pure states, and can
never be in this scrambled world. "Nationalism on this reading ... is a language of fantasy and escape," and belonging
can be so intense that it offers reasons to kill.[22] At the end of
the Cold War, he foolishly believed that the world could be
run by philosophers and poets; now he admits that

> liberal civilisation—the rule of laws not men,
> of argument in place of force, of compromise
> in place of violence—runs deeply against the
> human grain and is only achieved and

sustained by the most unremitting struggle
against human nature. The liberal virtues—
tolerance, compromise, reason—remain as
valuable as ever, but they cannot be preached to
those who are mad with fear or mad with
vengeance. In any case, preaching always rings
hollow. We must be prepared to defend them
by force, and the failure of the sated, cosmopolitan nations to do so has left the hungry
nations sick with contempt for us.[23]

Ethnic Wars

In *The Warrior's Honor: Ethnic War and the Modern Conscience*
(1998), Ignatieff renews his reflections on the moral obliga-
tion to assist strangers and the nature of modern war. He
begins optimistically, "There is no reason to despair. For
every society like Afghanistan mired in ethnic conflict, there
is a South Africa making its arduous journey back from the
abyss." He insists that "the world is not becoming more
chaotic or violent, although our failure to understand and act
makes it seem so." Over the last fifty years "our moral imagination has been transformed … by the growth of a language
and practice of moral universalism, expressed above all in a
shared human rights culture."[24]

In the book's second chapter, "The Narcissism of Minor
Difference," Ignatieff returns to a theme introduced in *Blood
and Belonging.* He adapts a Freudian insight to describe why
closely related individuals or groups can turn so ferociously
against each other. When self-love turns to aggression
against others (whatever may be the source of dispute), self-
identity must be emphasized and distinction from the enemy

must be exaggerated. "For this purpose, traditions are invented, a glorious past is gilded and refurbished for public consumption, and a people who might not have thought of themselves as a people at all suddenly begin to dream of themselves as a nation."[25] As self-absorption and distrust of others grows, "group pride in one group is bound to activate it in another." Tolerance becomes intolerance, but it can still be contained if groups live within "an overarching state" able to impose order and security.[26] If authority loses its strength, then distrust, hatred, fear, and paranoia take over. Mankind's inclination to violence, he sees, is a joint product of the common desire for personal safety and the absence of Thomas Hobbes's protective sovereign power to impose order. Ignatieff rejects Samuel Huntington's claim (and that of others) that the source of the Yugoslav wars is deep-seated, historic, unrelenting religious differences "that require only an infusion of fear to stir them into life." His own experience of those wars reveals a paradox: "True, gunners on each side made a particular point of targeting the churches, minarets, mosques, and burial grounds of the other side. But what is striking is the inauthenticity, shallowness, and fraudulence of their religious convictions. The militiamen I talked to said they were defending their families; they never once said they were defending their faith."[27] These targeted symbols of faith did not reflect the causes of war, but its manufactured excuses. (Though Ignatieff's judgement in this case may underestimate the symbolic significance of destroying the social institutions of the enemy; and his theory of ethnic conflict certainly underrates the influence of history and the perception of conflicting interests.)

Ignatieff takes pains to insist that, while much of modern

nationalist rhetoric may be misleading fantasy, not all of it is. Modern identities are often under threat; many minorities have been persecuted and denied the right to speak for themselves. "What is wrong with nationalism," he writes, "is not the desire to be master in your own house, but the conviction that only people like yourself deserve to be in the house."[28]

Instead, Ignatieff sees that his own liberalism depends on another fiction, another abstraction, another commitment of faith: that beneath the apparent differences of class, gender, colour, wealth, religion, and talent, which we can observe around us, lies a single humanity shared by all. "We are first and foremost juridical subjects, first and foremost citizens, equally entitled to a range of practices and protections; all differences are minor, and if they confer advantage, should be strenuously opposed."[29] This is the liberalism of tolerance and civic nationalism, requiring the acceptance of all citizens primarily as individuals, not as members of any group or class.

Liberal values require multiethnic and democratic societies for their fulfillment. But they also require peace and order for their maintenance, because wayward human beings—the real persons who live on all our streets, not the abstractions treated in laws and constitutions—will abandon respect for others in their search for self-protection if the state's authority disintegrates. The failed states of the 1990s offer a stark demonstration of this truth. Western nations and the web of international organizations that emerged after the Second World War have made their formal commitments to universal human rights. But who should impose the order necessary to apply those rights when order has disappeared? By the end of the century, Ignatieff accepted that his liberal good intentions could give him no answer, nor could the Charter of the

United Nations designed in 1945 to make the sovereign
borders of states inviolate. Lester Pearson and his United
Nations colleagues had devised a means in 1956 by which
parties at war could invite guardians from abroad to stand
between them as peacekeepers. But when order collapsed
within states, where was the Leviathan who could restore it?

In Sarajevo, Srebrenica, and Rwanda, the United Nations
Security Council showed that it could not do so. Ignatieff,
the anguished international reporter, took to the road once
more in 1995 to observe the devastating results of those failures. He writes angrily of a conversation with UN
Secretary-General Boutros Boutros-Ghali in the cabin of a
UN executive jet, heading south from Cairo to Rwanda. He
speaks of Srebrenica, where seven thousand men and boys
had been led away from a few Dutch soldiers in blue helmets
and murdered in the woods at the order of the Bosnian-Serb
army commander. Ignatieff tells us that Boutros-Ghali

> … once vowed to defend the "safe haven," but
> the Dutch, who have peacekeepers on the
> ground, vetoed further air strikes …
>
> At least forty thousand soldiers were needed
> to mount a credible defense of the safe havens.
> Only seven thousand were made available by
> the member states. I cannot make out whether
> the secretary-general believes that, with so few
> resources, a defense was even possible.
>
> Why call them safe havens if they were never
> safe? Why call UNPROFOR a protection force
> when it cannot protect itself? And why insist on
> being neutral, in the face of a clear aggressor
> and a clear victim, when that neutrality daily

undermines the United Nations' moral credit?

"We are not able to intervene on one side," Boutros-Ghali replies. "The mandate does not allow it."[30]

Ignatieff travelled with the UN secretary-general from Rwanda to Angola to Zaire to Burundi, meeting UN delegates in each of these battle zones and urging local leaders to accept their responsibilities. "If you don't," Boutros-Ghali tells them, "nobody will save you."[31] Looking back on this trip in 1998, Ignatieff sees the time as "the moment when liberal internationalism reached the end of its tether. The twin catastrophes of Srebrenica and Rwanda brought to a close a brief period of hope that had opened up in 1989." By then all nations were formally committed to a single international "human rights culture"; powerful international agencies could influence governments to do good abroad; television had brought the faces of human misery into every Western home; and jet transport "made us conscious, as we have never been before, that we *can* do something—and quickly—about the disasters we see on television."[32] The world's conscience was aroused, and a wave of humanitarian interventions took place under United Nations sponsorship in Cambodia, Kuwait, Kurdish Iraq, Somalia, and Bosnia. But three years after his African journey, Ignatieff saw international retreat and disillusionment.

Liberal internationalism had "reached the end of its tether." While others shared this gloomy thought, his words seem to be the particular expression of his own personal crisis of faith. A noble ideal had not matched his hard experience of the real world: "… a liberal interventionist foreign policy may be a contradiction in terms: principle commits us to intervene and yet forbids the imperial ruthlessness required to make interventionism succeed."[33]

In Iraq after Kuwait in 1991, he reflects, "we might have been a trifle more effective" if General Schwarzkopf had acted like a ruthless imperialist by marching on Baghdad and deposing Hussein; or in Somalia, if the US Marines had stayed in Mogadishu instead of withdrawing under attack; or in Bosnia, if NATO air strikes had crushed the Serbian rising in 1992; or again in Bosnia, if Western governments had forcefully taken the entire administration of Bosnia into their own hands under UN mandate in 1995.[34]

Moreover, Ignatieff accuses the very authors of the UN's operations of the 1990s (and perhaps himself as well) of moralistic hypocrisy. He identifies the guilty party with the collective "we":

> ... when policy was driven by moral motives, it was often driven by narcissism. We intervened not only to save others, but to save ourselves, or rather an image of ourselves as defenders of universal decencies. We wanted to show that the West "meant" something. This imaginary West, this narcissistic image of ourselves, we believed was incarnated in the myth of a multi-ethnic, multiconfessional Bosnia. The desire to intervene may have caused us to rewrite the history of Bosnia to make it conform to our ideal of a redeemable place.[35]

On the other hand, he now sees that when effective American involvement in Bosnia came after the outrage of Srebrenica (and ending with the signing of the Dayton peace accords), the intervention resulted from President Clinton's "political and geo-strategic" calculations, not from any sense of moral outrage. The new-born cynic coolly recognizes what he could not see before: "Clinton intervened in Bosnia to preserve his alliances, and to do so on American terms."[36] Who were "we"? Whose policies had been driven by moral motives and failed? It is difficult, here, to sort out Ignatieff's understanding of who was acting from what motives or in whose interests. Only the liberal interventionists, it seems, had been deceived about what was really going on, and Ignatieff had now, apparently, renounced that faith for clear-sighted realism.

As he continued to reflect on the internationalist failures of the 1990s (and even to exaggerate them, for there had been measured UN successes in Cambodia, Bosnia, Angola, and other places, as he later concedes), Ignatieff noticed that liberal intervention had involved an unexamined "assumption of omnipotence." We needed more humility.

> If we had started from more humble assumptions—that we can always do less than we would like, that we may be able to stop horror, but we cannot always prevent tragedy—we might have been more responsible and, just possibly, devised strategies of intervention that would have stood more of a chance of success.[37]

The call for humility, however, contradicted his previous suggestion that "imperial ruthlessness" might have produced more effective outcomes in Kuwait, Somalia, and Bosnia. Which choice was he recommending?

Instead, the UN's failures, he believed, had prompted

widespread moral disgust and disillusionment. The world
was no longer making sense, and that meant the disappear-
ance of any good reasons for moral engagement with it.

In 1998, Ignatieff had not come to that point of disen-
gagement. Between accepting that not much can be done
for the misfortunes of the world (on one side), and believing that there is so much more to do (on the other), he
searches for middle ground "where the ethics of commitment meets the ethics of responsibility, where the
commitments we make to strangers in danger can be
backed up by achievable strategies of rescue." He seeks
some reasonable rules of engagement. When should external military force be used in civil wars? When should
minority claims for secession be supported from abroad?
How can civil populations be protected from the effects of
civil war?[38]

To the first question, Ignatieff replies with a prudential
rather than a moral rule: since democratic electorates will
only permit low-risk intervention, while offending states will
only succumb to decisive force, "discriminate and targeted
intervention—through airpower" is the only practical
response. (This was what had brought the Serbs to the
bargaining table in Bosnia.) But preventive deployment of
ground troops *before* a civil war may actually stop it, so that,
too, is a reasonable option—and if so, the earlier the better.[39]
(Perhaps because there cannot be any useful general answer
to this first question, about the circumstances of intervention, he does not attempt to answer it. Instead, he suggests
how it should occur.)

On the second question—when to support claims to
secession—Ignatieff sees issues both of substance and timing.
There must be a "history of bad blood" and a "distinct and

recent memory of spilled blood," as well as a reasonable claim that the territory "is defensible and economically viable," and support should take place at a tipping point in the conflict when violence might still be minimized. These conditions, he notes, would rule out international support for any claim to Quebec independence. In Yugoslavia, Western governments failed in advance to set out any humane terms under which secession might be acceptable and then, when federal Yugoslavia attacked secessionist Slovenia and Croatia, waited too long and offered too little in coming to their aid.[40]

To the third question, on the protection of civilians, he offers another cautious reply with the example of Yugoslavia in mind. "In effect, the West's policy consisted of saying this: We will not fight the chief aggressor, and we will not enable the victims to resist, but we will try to prevent the victims from being wiped out."[41] The UN sent in a neutral protection force, he says, and found itself administering the brutal Serbian siege of Sarajevo. Nevertheless, it probably prevented the total conquest of Croatia and Bosnia by Serbian armies. At the same time, peacekeepers on the ground became potential hostages and prevented the use of effective UN air power. This particular effort to protect civilians was a tragic failure. Acting under an inadequate mandate, the UN eventually gained only a scorched battleground and its wounded inhabitants.

Thus, Ignatieff offers no satisfactory answers to any of his three questions about international intervention in failed states. When he responds with generalities, they cannot cover the complex conditions that history actually throws up. When he responds from a particular case, he can only "ask whether, in the end, they didn't make things worse."[42]

For the future he offers more generalizations. They are

superficially constructive (or at least well-meaning) but
border on platitudes:

> What these societies need is internal peace
> followed by the construction of institutions in
> which the rule of law rather than the rule of
> the gun prevails. This is work that is totally ill
> suited to the post–Cold War style of instant
> intervention and quick exit. What is needed is
> long-term, unspectacular commitment to the
> rebuilding of society itself. Obviously, such
> enduring work can be undertaken only by the
> people themselves, but an enduring commit-
> ment by outsiders can help.[43]

Although there are kernels of undeveloped policy in this
statement, Ignatieff's narrative hovers between vagueness,
nostalgia, and despair. He recalls Joseph Conrad's *Heart of
Darkness* as a fable of "vile imperial rule," yet he also reflects
that those nineteenth-century empires of the Europeans and
the Ottoman Turks "had a certain logic: Those who cannot
agree to rule themselves may be able to submit to rule by
strangers."[44] Humanitarian conscience, he suggests, has
proven itself too weak as a link between the flourishing
states of this century and the cast-off, failed states of former
empire. The old commercial and strategic ties between
imperial centres and their colonies were stronger and
perhaps more humane than those conjured up by well-
intentioned liberal internationalists at the United Nations.

By the dawn of the twenty-first century, Ignatieff had
become convinced that the problem of war, "in most of the
danger zones of the post–Cold War world, is the disintegra-

tion of states."[45] The police and armies of nation-states—whether they come from within or from without as enforcers—are the only bodies able to deal with "large-scale human violence."[46] This insight, when accompanied by his hint about the advantages of empires, seemed to be moving the passionate advocate of human rights in a surprising direction.

Kosovo and Humanitarian Interventionism

In 1999, the next European war provided a test case for Ignatieff's emerging view that serious and continuing violations of human rights within a state justified military intervention from abroad. He chronicled that case, and his support for the intervention, in *Virtual War: Kosovo and Beyond* (2000). The case of Kosovo seemed to match Ignatieff's arguments almost perfectly, and those arguments equally matched the justifications for war made by the alliance that attacked Serbia in March 1999. The leaders of that alliance were the United States (under President Clinton), Great Britain (under Prime Minister Blair), and the other members of the North Atlantic Treaty Organization (including Canada).

When the Bosnian war came to an end in 1995, the negotiators at Dayton, Ohio made a tactical decision (under pressure from Serbia) to avoid dealing with the nationalist claims for independence already emerging from Yugoslavia's southern province of Kosovo. In return, Serbia's leader Slobodan Milosevic was repeatedly warned that if he hoped to avoid an ethnic war engulfing the entire region, his government would have to restore to Kosovo's Albanian Muslims the collective rights they had lost in 1989.[47] The peacemakers settled one war, and bought breathing space during which another one might, just possibly, be avoided. That was unlikely, because Milosevic had previously declared Kosovo to be the sacred birthplace of the Serbian nation. For three years, he failed to act on the warnings from Dayton, until Albanian guerrillas, operating under the name of the Kosovo Liberation Army (KLA), began raids against Serbian police and military units in the province. The Serbs retaliated with violent attacks on Kosovo villages, and tens of thousands of civilians fled into the mountains of western Kosovo. As violence spread, the United States took the lead in creating a Contact Group to exert pressure on Milosevic and inspired the creation of an unarmed international Verification Mission to monitor a tenuous ceasefire in the province.

As in other moments of tension, Ignatieff took himself to the centre of the action. In December 1998 he accompanied the American negotiator on Kosovo, Richard Holbrooke, to Belgrade, where Holbrooke would use his impressive skills to cajole and threaten Milosevic into retreat. Ignatieff admired Holbrooke as a tough and astute diplomat. Holbrooke brought with him an offer that would give Milosevic a three-year delay in talks on Kosovo's final status, in return for renewed Kosovo autonomy within Yugoslavia. The package would be sweetened with the promise of a NATO peace force to separate the combatants. But Holbrooke's nighttime meeting with Milosevic showed that diplomacy had come too late: both sides had abandoned any thought of compromise. The KLA aggressively insisted on full independence, while Milosevic had never been in any mood to deal away Serbia's birthplace. Holbrooke departed, and the killing continued on both sides.[48]

A month later, after a slaughter of forty-five civilians in the village of Racak by Serb paramilitaries and police, NATO's threats of air strikes against Serbia brought it to the bargaining table at Rambouillet in France. But there was no bargaining: the American secretary of state, Madeleine Albright, instead produced an ultimatum. While the Kosovo delegation accepted the American plan for autonomy under NATO protection, Serbia rejected the terms because they called, in effect, for foreign military occupation of both Kosovo and Serbia. The proposal seemed to be intended either to bring about Serbia's capitulation or to justify war following Milosevic's walkout. Whatever may have been Serbia's responsibility for the crimes in Kosovo, the Rambouillet affair was a crude piece of stage-management that was hardly understood by the public in North America or Europe. Richard Falk of Princeton University called it "the abandonment of diplomacy rather than a good-faith effort."[49] It cannot be interpreted as a failed "last resort" before a war entered into reluctantly as NATO's propaganda made it out to be.[50] Kosovo was a "war of choice" on the part of the United States and NATO; Rambouillet was its fig-leaf. Ignatieff does not describe the war this way, and in discussing its justifications he does not comment on how acceptance of Rambouillet would have undercut Serbian sovereignty beyond the boundaries of Kosovo. This omission from *Virtual War* is a grave one, perhaps only explicable on the ground that since Ignatieff had already accepted the need to violate Serbian sovereignty, it was preferable to see it done peacefully under threat of war rather than by war itself. But in that case, the offer made to Milosevic should have been persuasive enough for his serious consideration. It was not.

After the parties left Rambouillet, Serbian violence in Kosovo sharpened in intensity. There were two more fruitless diplomatic meetings, in Rambouillet and Paris; NATO began troop movements to Macedonia, on the southern border of Kosovo; Holbrooke travelled briefly again to Belgrade; and on March 24, 1999, NATO began what turned out to be an eleven-week aerial bombardment of Serbia.[51]

Once the bombing started, Serbia launched a prepared offensive of terror, probably called Operation Horseshoe, to expel the entire Albanian Muslim population of the province. This brazen act of criminality should have been foreseen by the NATO coalition, but apparently was not. Within a few weeks, over one million citizens were driven across the borders into Macedonia and Albania. At American insistence, the allied war plan against Kosovo failed to provide for quick intervention by mobile ground forces, which could easily have occupied key points in Kosovo, protected the population, and forestalled most of the expulsions. But after Vietnam and Somalia, Bill Clinton was not prepared to accept American casualties on the ground. As the deportees filled up the muddy fields of Macedonia and the relief agencies rushed in to cope, Ignatieff was there to sympathize with and interview the desperate exiles.[52]

An air war using high-tech precision bombing was the kind that Ignatieff had approved and predicted. Milosevic did not capitulate as expected, and world-wide television audiences watched daily as occasional Serbian tanks, Danube bridges, Serb military supply dumps, government ministries, electric power plants, oil refineries, state television studios, the Chinese embassy, and collateral Serb civilians were bombarded with high explosives, cluster bombs, and shells coated with depleted uranium. Throughout this onslaught from the skies, Serbian military strength in the province of Kosovo increased.

As international frustration and complaints mounted over the destructive stalemate, both sides buckled enough to bring about a ceasefire. Under both public and military pressure, the NATO coalition partners prepared to invade Kosovo with land forces from the south, and Milosevic chose his moment to make a bargain. At the end of May, as the Hague Tribunal indicted him for war crimes and the Russians warned that he would no longer have their diplomatic support, Milosevic accepted terms. Serbian forces would evacuate Kosovo, an autonomous provincial government would be restored, NATO forces would provide continuing protection in the province, the UN would accept oversight pending a delayed decision on Kosovo's permanent status, and the Milosevic government would survive to lick its wounds in Belgrade. Within two years, domestic political events brought about Milosevic's departure from office. He finally surrendered to the International Criminal Tribunal at the Hague and died during trial early in 2006.

One month into the Kosovo War, Prime Minister Blair spoke to the Economic Club of Chicago to offer his justification for the war.[53] "While we meet here in Chicago this evening," he said, "unspeakable things are happening in Europe. Awful crimes that we never thought we would see again have reappeared—ethnic cleansing, systematic rape, mass murder." These were the responsibility of the Milosevic dictatorship, and they had to be fought.

This is a just war, based not on any territorial ambitions but on values. We cannot let the evil of ethnic cleansing stand. We must not rest until it is reversed. We have learned twice before in this century that appeasement does not work. If we let an evil dictator range unchallenged, we will have to spill infinitely more blood and treasure to stop him later.

Prime Minister Blair placed the war within a context of global interdependence, American power, and what he saw as a shift in international moral values. Kosovo pointed to a longer-term agenda. Many of the world's current problems, he said, "have been caused by two dangerous and ruthless men—Saddam Hussein and Slobodan Milosevic. Both have been prepared to wage vicious campaigns against sections of their own community. As a result of these destructive policies, both have brought calamity on their own peoples ... One of the reasons why it is now so important to win the conflict is to ensure that others do not make the same mistake in the future."

Blair argued that after the end of the Cold War, "a new framework" of ideas was required for NATO:

No longer is our existence as states under threat. Now our actions are guided by a more subtle blend of mutual self interest and moral purpose in defending the values we cherish. In the end values and interests merge. If we can establish and spread the values of liberty, the rule of law, human rights and an open society then that is in our

national interests too. The spread of our
values makes us safer. As John Kennedy put
it "Freedom is indivisible and when one man
is enslaved who is free?"

Since free nations could not take on the burden of right-
ing all the world's wrongs, they would have to define the
circumstances when they should try. It was reasonable and
practical, he conceded, for nations to accept the traditional
rule of non-interference as the norm, but there had to be
limits. He named two basic justifications for intervention:
acts of genocide and oppression that "produces massive
flows of refugees which unsettle neighbouring countries."
Given those offences, he suggested a checklist of five
conditions to be satisfied before any military attack from
abroad: 1. "Are we sure of our case?" 2. "Have we
exhausted all the diplomatic options?" 3. "On the basis of a
practical assessment of the situation, are there military
operations we can sensibly and prudently undertake?" 4.
"Are we prepared for the long term?" 5. "And finally, do we
have national interests involved?" In Kosovo he was
convinced that these conditions had been met. "I am not
suggesting that these are absolute tests," Blair added with
the humility suitable to the author of a new set of holy
commandments. "But they are the kind of issues we need
to think about in deciding in the future when and whether
we will intervene."

Blair admitted that the new rules would only work within
a reformed United Nations and under the leadership of the
world's strongest state, which "has no dreams of world
conquest and is not seeking colonies." He addressed a plea
and an assurance to his American audience:

I say to you: never fall again for the doctrine of
isolationism. The world cannot afford it. Stay
a country, outward-looking, with the vision
and imagination that is your nature. And
realise that in Britain you have a friend and an
ally that will stand with you, work with you,
fashion with you the design of a future built on
peace and prosperity for all, which is the only
dream that makes humanity worth preserving.

The speech came close to Ignatieff's views. He approved
of it and echoed its phrases.[54]

When Ignatieff calculated the moral and legal balance
in favour of the military campaign against Serbia in
Kosovo, he argued that the international standard for a
state's behaviour had been established by the Nuremberg
trials and the Universal Declaration of Human Rights.
Armed intervention, he suggested, could be justified if
Blair's two preconditions had been satisfied: "[F]irst, when
human rights abuses rise to the level of a systematic
attempt to expel or exterminate large numbers of people
who have no means of defending themselves; second,
where these abuses threaten the peace and security of
neighboring states." He added two conditions from Blair's
checklist: that all diplomatic options had been exhausted
and that force had "a real chance of working ... In my
view," he concluded, "Kosovo does meet the strict criteria
for a justified intervention."[55]

In June 1999, Ignatieff's challenger in a dialogue on the
war, the liberal writer and life peer Robert Skidelsky, denied
in *Prospect* magazine that the war could be justified.[56] The
United Nations, he recalled, had been founded on respect

for national sovereignty for good prudential reasons, with the sole limitation that legal sanctions might be applied when states threaten international peace. There were no agreed international standards for judging such threats, and in the Kosovo case, no authority had been sought for intervention from the UN Security Council. While Skidelsky noted that Ignatieff conceded a "general presumption" in favour of non-intervention, "… you qualify this so heavily as almost to turn it into its opposite." Skidelsky centred his opposition to Ignatieff's case on two central points. First, he suggested that Ignatieff's argument about the exodus of Kosovars out of Yugoslavia was upside-down: "Historians will argue about whether Milosevic's savage reprisals against the KLA turned into a deliberate program of ethnic cleansing. What is undeniable is that the mass exodus from Yugoslavia started after the bombing started. I would have expected more skepticism from you about NATO's claims." Second, he protested that NATO bombing of Yugoslavia was not a "credible way to stop abuses and restore peace." On the contrary, "the NATO action has made the world a more dangerous place."

Ignatieff responded to Skidelsky with a series of assertions. There were, he insisted, accepted international standards for military intervention "in the face of more than twelve years of increasing Serbian repression"; members of the NATO alliance alone should not be held to the terms of the UN Charter when "the list of UN resolutions which Milosevic has ignored or violated is exceedingly long"; Milosevic's ethnic cleansing "was underway in Kosovo ten months before the bombing began. The departure of the Kosovar Albanians was not an 'exodus,' but systematic deportation, using military units."

But Ignatieff conceded significant doubts about NATO's bombing campaign and its failure to introduce ground troops into Kosovo. "I framed my conditions for the use of military force in the belief that force can only be justified if it achieves precise military objectives." If Milosevic agreed to negotiate a return of the refugees to their homes "under international protection," then the bombing should immediately stop. If he did not, then bombing should continue to prepare for a ground invasion, the defeat and withdrawal of Serb armies from the province, the return of refugees, and the rebuilding of Kosovo under UN supervision. "A bombing campaign which is not geared to this objective, and which simply continues to destroy the infrastructure of Serbia and kill civilians, would have nobody's support in the long term. The bombing must be directed at military targets with the aim of introducing ground troops as soon as possible."

These were a writer's easy pieties, but they also reflected growing popular feeling and debate in NATO countries and among Western war planners. Finally, Ignatieff told Skidelsky that "the fact which you do not wish to face is that every peaceful diplomatic alternative to the war was tried and failed. Why? Because Milosevic gambled that we would fold. And you seem to wish that we had. The word for this is appeasement."[57] In the midst of battle, this was a sly British accusation with a long history.

The evidence about Serbia's actions and intentions towards the Kosovar population in 1999 remains a matter of contention and uncertainty. Was there in fact ground for Ignatieff's assertion that the major expulsions were not primarily a response to NATO's aerial attacks? (Later Ignatieff was ambiguous on this central point.[58]) It was certainly true that in Milosevic's earlier campaigns in

Croatia and Bosnia, his armies had initiated crude actions of ethnic cleansing. But whether NATO was responding to facts or engaging in a pre-emptive war, the great bulk of the forced expulsions did occur after the bombing had begun. Up to this point, the UN's acceptance that pre-emptive wars were illegitimate under international law had been taken for granted, if not always recognized in practice. Now, the principle was openly flouted by two great powers.

The weakest parts of Ignatieff's defence of the war relate not to the acts of Milosevic and his armies before the NATO bombings, but to what happened after the war began. As he might admit, the allied attack brought immense, long-term suffering to the Kosovars and to the whole population of Serbia. Ignatieff's condition that "force can only be justified when it stands a real chance of working" cannot easily survive the history of the war and its aftermath. Did it "work"? The evidence for failure is powerful: over a million refugees displaced, many civilians killed, the social and economic infrastructure of both Kosovo and Serbia wrecked, Milosevic still in command of Serbia (though politically weakened), and a barely controlled new wave of ethnic cleansing underway in Kosovo (this time directed against the minority Serb population of the province). These are hardly minor events to be ignored when looking for useful lessons in the war or balancing the moral accounts.

When he met the NATO commander, General Wesley Clark, two weeks after the end of the stalemated war, Ignatieff asked him whether the air campaign had worked. Thirty-four thousand air sorties over seventy-eight days had not cowed Milosevic's field forces, whose armoured regiments had withdrawn defiantly from Kosovo in June under orders from Belgrade, "making obscene gestures at the Western camera crews" as they passed. Clark could not say why the undefeated armies had been withdrawn.

" 'You'd have to ask Milosevic and he'll never tell you,' Clark replied."[59] He explained the failure of NATO's strategy as the outcome of complex internal diplomacy that was needed to sustain the campaign for so long among the coalition's nineteen partners. But Ignatieff called Clark "the man who won the first postmodern war in history."[60]

Shortly after his meeting with General Clark, Ignatieff returned to Belgrade to meet old friends in the wounded city. After long conversations, he could recognize the moral ambiguity of his support for the war, but the Yugoslavs were still struggling with the breakup of a multi-ethnic state while his community in Western Europe and North America had come to accept the need for multi-ethnic societies. This imagined superiority, he wrote,

> … was what held the West together in its stand against Serbian ethnic cleansing. And it was this self-approving moral image which seemed so false to the Serbs. Who were *we* to tell them how to live with their minorities? Who were we to preach tolerance? And who were we to bomb them when their leaders refused to capitulate?
>
> The only honest answer to these arguments is that they are an example of moral perfectionism. The requirement that "he who casts the first stone should be without sin" is a guarantee of inaction. The fact that the West does not live up to its ideals does not invalidate the ideals or invalidate their defense. Ideals are frequently

defended by people with dirty hands—and bad
consciences. That is what our argument came
down to—bad consciences on both sides.[61]

In admitting his sense of guilt, Ignatieff was certainly not
admitting that it had been wrong to go to war. Rather, he
was looking forward with Prime Minister Blair to further
adventures abroad in defence of his ideals.

But Ignatieff was covering his tracks as he went. Using
human rights violations to justify going to war, Ignatieff
admitted in *Virtual War*, is morally risky. "Those who
supported the Kosovo War must face up to the unintended
effects of moralizing the use of violence. For high-flown
abstractions carry an inherent justification of everything
done in their name. What is to prevent moral abstractions
like human rights from inducing an absolutist frame of
mind which, in defining all human rights violators as
barbarians, legitimizes barbarism?"[62] Those who make such
claims, he warns, must be sure that in acting they do not
destroy what they set out to save. They must see themselves
and their enemies as they are, as persons, not as fabled
warriors on one side or hateful tyrants on the other. "Only
then can we get our hands dirty. Only then can we do what
is right."[63]

Or perhaps not even then. By the end of *Virtual War*, I
defy any reader to work out what message is being delivered.
Ignatieff's argument is a display of wordplay. On the surface
the lesson seems to be that modern high-tech precision air
warfare reported in real time on television (as in the Kosovo
War) is actually being used to deceive its audiences, either to
make them believe that it is all a harmless video game or that
it is too deadly to support. (Ignatieff suggests, for example,

that the killing of Serbian television staff by American guided bombs can be blamed on the Serbians, who intentionally kept staff in the studios to provide victims whose deaths could be reported.) Whichever it is, the public may be disenchanted by what it sees and want it to stop. But that does not mean, for Ignatieff, that it *should* stop: for after all, the enemy that provoked the war could be the evil tyrant that propaganda made him out to be. The real lessons, the subliminal lessons, of the book seem to be that the democratic leaders of Western nations must more effectively control the TV messages that reach their publics during wartime and that those leaders must defy any popular sentiments of humanity that could temper their ruthless resolve to win. They must be able to complete what they set out to do. *Virtual War* turns out to be an essay on the justification of war, rather than a sermon by a human rights specialist on its moral dangers. The complexity of the argument, however, gives Ignatieff plenty of scope to deny this claim. The message is more likely to get through to the communications experts advising a British prime minister or an American president than to a perplexed citizen trying to work his or her way through the maze of words.

CHAPTER 2

War without End

After *Virtual War* Ignatieff turned from reporting, media analysis, and philosophical polemic to academic writing on the theory and practice of human rights. In this field he had a considerable international reputation. In *Human Rights as Politics and Idolatry* (2003), he notes that after the Second World War "individuals—regardless of race, creed, gender, age, or any other status—were granted rights that they could use to challenge unjust state law or oppressive customary practice."[64] This "rights revolution" has, among other things, challenged the principle of inviolate state sovereignty: "… in practice the exercise of state sovereignty is conditional, to some degree, on observance of proper human rights behavior. When states fail in this regard, they render themselves subject to criticism, sanction, and, as a final resort, intervention."[65]

At the core of this book is a discussion of the legitimacy of military intervention in areas "where all order … has disintegrated and its people have been delivered up to a war of all against all, or where a state is engaging in gross, repeated, and systematic violence against its own citizens …"[66] A few months after the end of the Kosovo War, Ignatieff vigorously defended Clinton and Blair against charges that allied propaganda leading up to the war had exaggerated the scale of

Serbia's pre-war killing in Kosovo in order to justify intervention. He rejected the claims as "not proven," but said that the real issue was "not about numbers." What critics called "oppression," he called "atrocity." What threshold, he asked, was necessary "before we send in the planes and the troops? ... The true lesson of Kosovo," he suggested, was that foreign troops and bombers should have gone into the province nine months earlier, in the summer of 1998, "to convince Mr. Milosevic that we knew where the line was between oppression and massacre, even if he did not."[67]

Since 1991, Ignatieff reports, governments have claimed a "right of humanitarian intervention" in Haiti, Somalia, Iraq, Bosnia, and Kosovo, even though "the juridical status of a right of intervention is exceedingly unclear." The UN Charter forbids the invasion of national sovereignty while also proclaiming human rights; the Universal Declaration of 1948 and later covenants imply the right of intervention, but do not establish it in international law (except within the European community). States have been reluctant to apply the right and have only done so temporarily, without claiming that sovereignty has been permanently overridden. As examples, Ignatieff mentions Kurdish Northern Iraq—then under British-American air protection without any formal denial of Iraqi sovereignty—and Kosovo, under UN protection while it remains formally a part of Yugoslavia. States cling to the principle of sovereignty, he suggests, partly "to prevent intervention from becoming imperial," despite the fact of several recent long-term occupations.[68]

Ignatieff doubts that these post–Cold War interventions have been either successful or consistent. Because they were entered into on the assumption that they were temporary, the participants did not expect them to achieve any long-term stability. On the other hand, he insists that standing aside is no alternative: the Rwandan genocide of 1994 did even more to undermine belief in human rights claims. "So what are we to do?" he asks. "If human rights are universal, human rights abuses everywhere are our business. But we simply cannot intervene everywhere. If we do not ration our resources, how can we possibly be effective? Rationing is both inevitable and necessary, yet there needs to be a clear basis to justify these decisions."[69]

Echoing the Kosovo doctrine defined by Blair, Ignatieff suggests that there are three conditions "for the rationing of interventions": "gross, systematic and pervasive" abuses; threats to international peace; and real prospects of stopping the abuses. And he adds a fourth limiting "condition," which is a recognition of reality rather than a rule of intervention: that a great power must have vital interests in the region which are not challenged by any other great power. In the case of Kosovo, he claims, the vital interest of NATO was "to demonstrate the credibility of NATO when faced with a challenge from a defiant leader of a small state."[70]

When no power has a vital interest in intervention, it will not occur. Of course, vital interests are imprecise things. The scale of abuses, or the possibility that they will infect border states—as in Rwanda—"may be so terrible that we are bound to intervene even when they do not impinge on any direct national interest."[71]

Ignatieff's rules for intervention, taken together, seem to be simply prudential guidelines or realistic predictions, rather than moral imperatives. Certainly there was no international consensus in 2001 authorizing their use. They stem from the example of Kosovo, when a few nations led a reluctant North Atlantic Treaty Organization into the operation. During the war, the coalition remained so tenuous that members squabbled throughout the campaign and made separate decisions on whether to participate in some of NATO's bombing missions. How were the rules established, except by fiat of Prime Minister Blair (as modified by Ignatieff) delivered in the midst of war? And who would interpret them in the next crisis?

Such an uncertain set of rules and practices on military intervention, Ignatieff reports, is defended by some states because a bias in favour of non-intervention serves to protect them from attack by larger states. Others call for a shift in the balance away from respect for sovereignty and towards the right of intervention: in their view, when human rights are abused "the Security Council should have the right to mandate a graduated set of coercive responses ranging from sanctions to full-scale military intervention. The failure to formalize a right of intervention under the UN system," he continues, "simply means that coalitions of the willing who wish to intervene will do so by bypassing the authorizing process of the United Nations altogether."[72] This, he concedes, is what will actually happen, since there is no chance that the UN could agree on more formal rules for forceful interventions. "Human rights may be universal, but support for coercive enforcement of their norms will never be universal. Because interventions will lack full legitimacy, they will have to be limited and partial, and as a result, they will be only partially successful."[73]

By default, Ignatieff has fallen back on the admission that intervention will in fact occur at the whim of the major powers. Yet he continues to believe in the need for such intervention. The logic of his position is that, when severe abuses occur, diplomatic attention should be directed at persuading great powers (or *a* great power) to act militarily, rather than attempting the impossible at the United Nations. His implied change of diplomatic focus might well mean that broader, multilateral approaches to the avoidance of crises would be ignored.

Ignatieff rightly notes that the currency of human rights has been devalued by the UN's failure to honour its promises of protection in Rwanda and Srebrenica. In these disasters, the United Nations mistakenly viewed itself as a neutral peacekeeper, when success would have required it to intervene "only as part of peace-enforcement operations in which the international community aligns with the side more nearly in the right and uses military force robustly to stop human rights abuse and create conditions for the reestablishment of stable state order in the region."[74] He sees, as well, that in Kosovo the moral copybook has been stained by all sides. The Muslim KLA committed atrocities, knowing that these would provoke Serbian reprisals, which eventually led to the Western military intervention against the Serbs, but the NATO military attack "then unleashed a genuine human rights disaster: the forcible eviction of 800,000 Kosovan citizens to Albania and Macedonia, followed by the massacre of up to 10,000 of those who remained."[75]

This was only the beginning of the coalition's moral dilemmas. Kosovars felt betrayed that their pains did not earn them statehood, while the West felt betrayed that liberation of the province was followed by a new round of evictions of local Serbs. "An indefinite UN protectorate in Kosovo seems the only solution," he suggested, "since it postpones the necessity of deciding Kosovo's final status. Yet an indefinite protectorate amounts to imperialism, and this violates the anti-imperial ethos of our human rights commitment."[76] For Ignatieff, the only conclusion consistent with "our principles" is eventual political independence for Kosovo, beyond international supervision: "Either we believe that people should rule themselves or we do not. A prolonged imperial administration of the south Balkans, justified in the name of human rights, will actually end up violating the very principles it purports to defend."[77]

Beyond calling for this commitment to moral consistency, Ignatieff judges that "we" or "the West" (those he believes are the responsible actors in the human rights drama, who are not always clearly defined in his prose) must find a means "to apply human rights criteria to the strong as well as to the weak," and somehow work out how "to reconcile individual human rights with our commitment to self-determination and state sovereignty."[78] He offers no immediate suggestions for achieving these difficult goals.

After admitting that he expects no more than minimal gains in the world campaign for human rights, Ignatieff's final words in *Human Rights as Politics and Idolatry* are these:

> We may not be able to create democracies or constitutions. Liberal freedom may be some way off. But we could do more than we do to stop unmerited suffering and gross physical cruelty. That I take to be the elemental priority of all human rights activism: to stop torture, beatings, killings, rape, and assault and to improve, as best we can, the security of ordinary people.[79]

Rules for Intervention: The Kosovo Commission

For many supporters as well as critics of the Kosovo War, the way this "humanitarian intervention" occurred and the way it was fought left pain, frustration, and uncertainty. In the aftermath, Prime Minister Goran Perrson of Sweden proposed an inquiry on the war, and in August 1999 he announced the appointment of Justice Richard Goldstone of South Africa and Carl Tham of Sweden as co-chairs of an Independent International Commission on Kosovo.[80] Eleven other commissioners were appointed for a one-year term by the chair and co-chair "on the basis of known expertise." They included Dr. Hanan Ashrawi (an independent politician and academic from Palestine), Richard Falk and Martha Minow (international and human rights law professors from the United States), Mary Kaldor (an international affairs professor from the United Kingdom), and Michael Ignatieff, along with members from Germany, Benin, Japan, Russia, France, and the Czech Republic. Here was an opportunity for Ignatieff to make his case for rules that could legitimize intervention when human rights disasters occur. After a year of meetings, seminars, and consultations, the commission presented its report (as a courtesy) to UN Secretary-General Kofi Annan in October 2000.

The commission ranged widely over the causes, nature, and results of the war, focusing particularly on violations of human rights, the justification for military intervention, the problem of establishing criteria for intervention, the roles of NATO and the United Nations, the future of Kosovo, and the lessons to be learned by all parties. These were all issues that Ignatieff had helped to define in his previous writings.

The report of the commission, in its turn, shaped Ignatieff's subsequent approach to the problems of "humanitarian interventionism."

The commission found an appalling record of irreconcilable goals, failed diplomacy, wartime atrocities, strategic and tactical errors, and postwar confusion in the affair. Four hundred thousand Kosovars had left or been driven from their homes in the year before the NATO campaign began; 863,000 civilians had fled the country during the three months of war (most of them expelled by Yugoslav forces); 569,000 more were internally displaced, and 10,000 civilians killed (mostly by Yugoslav troops). The commission added:

> There is also evidence of widespread rape and torture, as well as looting, pillaging and extortion. The pattern of the logistical arrangements … shows that this huge expulsion of Kosovo-Albanians was systematic and deliberately organized. The NATO air campaign did not provoke the attacks on the civilian Kosovar population but the bombing created an environment that made such an operation feasible.[81]

The pre-war phase of diplomacy was so confused that the commission could find no clear lessons for the future, "beyond the prudential observations in favor of early engagement and greater attentiveness to nonviolent options." The NATO intervention, the commission concluded, was "illegal but legitimate."

> It was illegal because it did not receive prior approval from the United Nations Security

Council. However, the Commission considers that the intervention was justified because all diplomatic avenues had been exhausted and because the intervention had the effect of liberating the majority population of Kosovo from a long period of oppression under Serbian rule.[82]

NATO made "a major mistake" in believing that Milosevic would capitulate in the face of a short bombing campaign and "underestimated the obvious risk" of a Serbian attack on Kosovar civilians. Despite efforts to avoid civilian casualties, 500 civilian deaths were documented and more were left under threat.

> The Commission is also critical of the use of cluster bombs, the environmental damage caused by the use of depleted-uranium tipped armor-piercing shells and missiles and by toxic leaks caused by the bombing of industrial and petroleum complexes in several cities, and the attack on Serbian television.[83]

The commission's final conclusions were blunt but even-handed:

> In conclusion, the NATO war was neither a success nor a failure; it was in fact both. It forced the Serbian government to withdraw its army and police from Kosovo and to sign an agreement closely modeled on the aborted Rambouillet accord. It stopped the systematic

oppression of the Kosovar Albanians. However, the intervention failed to achieve its avowed aim of preventing massive ethnic cleansing. Milosevic remained in power. The Serbian people were the main losers. Kosovo was lost. Many Serbs fled or were expelled from the province. Serbia suffered considerable economic losses and destruction of civilian infrastructure. Independent media and NGOs were suppressed and the overall level of repression in Serbia increased.[84]

For the future, the commission recommended "conditional independence" for Kosovo, outside Yugoslavia but "within an international framework" which would include a security guarantee and monitored protection of minority rights—all of this to be negotiated among a wide group of interested parties.[85] (By mid-2006, that process had not been completed; instead, the province remained under the UN trusteeship imposed in 1999.)

On military intervention, the commission judged that the time was ripe for the adoption of "a principled framework ... which could be used to guide future responses to imminent humanitarian catastrophes and which could be used to assess claims for humanitarian intervention." The commissioners hoped that the UN General Assembly would adopt such a declaration, and that the charter would be "adapted to" the declaration, either by amendment or by case-by-case application in the Security Council. Not surprisingly, the proposed framework consisted of the three principles already asserted by Blair and Ignatieff, along with eight "contextual principles" to be used to weigh "the degree of legitimacy possessed by the actual use of force." The report modestly conceded "the political problems of implementing such a change."[86] Despite his own previous skepticism, Ignatieff had endorsed an effort to place future military interventions within legal bounds. He thus chose a twin-track strategy: the idealist seeking approved rules of intervention, the realist expecting vigilante operations by coalitions of the willing at times and places of their own choice.

"The Responsibility to Protect"

In his Millennium Report to the United Nations General Assembly, Kofi Annan took up the appeal of the Kosovo Commission by challenging UN member states to face up to the moral, legal, and practical problems of humanitarian intervention. In September 2000, Canadian Prime Minister Jean Chrétien told the General Assembly that Canada would create an international commission to study the issues, and a week later Foreign Affairs Minister Lloyd Axworthy announced the creation of the International Commission on Intervention and State Sovereignty (ICISS). Canada was responding to Annan's challenge, he said, "to ensure that the indifference and inaction of the international community, in the face of such situations as occurred in Rwanda and Srebrenica, are no longer an option."[87] The commission would seek "to foster a global political consensus on how to move towards action within the UN system." It would be co-chaired by Gareth Evans of Australia and Mohamed Sahnoun of Algeria, acting with ten other commissioners, including two Canadians, Gisèle Côté-Harper (of Laval University) and Michael Ignatieff. (Ignatieff's appointment overlapped his membership on the Kosovo Commission, which was just completing its report). The inquiry was launched with a one-year mandate and was about to finish its work when the attacks of September 11, 2001, took place in New York and Washington. The shocking impact of these events was reflected in the commission's report, which was submitted to the UN Secretary General in December 2001.[88]

The report was linguistically ingenious. It succeeded in taming the threatening language of "humanitarian intervention" and the "right to intervene" by rechristening them more positively as "the responsibility to protect"; and it magically resolved the contradiction between state sovereignty and intervention by redefining sovereignty to include a responsibility to protect:

> The definition of state sovereignty, by even its strongest supporters, does not include any claim of unlimited power of a state to do what it wants to its own people ... It is acknowledged that sovereignty implies a dual responsibility: externally—to respect the sovereignty of other states, and internally, to respect the dignity and basic rights of all the people within the state. In international human rights covenants, in UN practice, and in state practice itself, sovereignty is now understood as embracing this dual responsibility. Sovereignty as responsibility has become the minimum content of good international citizenship.[89]

The commission recognized that there are widespread fears about acknowledging any "right to intervene" that includes possible military action, and thus held it necessary for the international community to develop "consistent, credible and enforceable standards to guide state and inter-governmental practice."[90] The report proposed a complex scheme of "core principles" and "principles for military intervention," which it asked the UN General Assembly to adopt in a "declaratory resolution," to be followed by actions of the Security Council and Secretary General giving it effect.[91] These principles amounted to an elaboration of the Blair and Ignatieff rules:

> Where a population is suffering serious harm, as a result of internal war, insurgency, repression or state failure, and the state in question is unwilling or unable to halt or avert it, the principle of non-intervention yields to the international responsibility to protect …
>
> Military intervention for human protection purposes is an exceptional and extraordinary measure. To be warranted, there must be serious and irreparable harm occurring to human beings, or imminently likely to occur, of the following kind:
>
> > A. large scale loss of life, actual or apprehended, with genocidal intent or not, which is the product either of deliberate state action, or state neglect or inability to act, or a failed state situation; or
> >
> > B. large scale "ethnic cleansing", actual or apprehended, whether carried out

by killing, forced expulsion, acts of
terror or rape.[92]

This "just cause threshold" was backed by four "precaution-
ary principles" derived from just war theory: "right intention
... to halt or avert human suffering"; "last resort ... with
reasonable grounds for believing lesser measures would not
have succeeded"; "proportional means ... scale, duration and
intensity should be the minimum necessary ..."; "and reasonable prospects ... of success ... with the consequences of action
not likely to be worse than the consequences of inaction."[93]
While the document proposed that the UN Security
Council should apply these terms, it warned of one possible
escape from the rules: "The Security Council should take into
account in all its deliberations that, if it fails to discharge its
responsibility to protect in conscience-shocking situations
crying out for action, concerned states may not rule out other
means to meet the gravity and urgency of that situation—and
that the stature and credibility of the United Nations may
suffer thereby."[94]
As a comprehensive effort to define the occasions when
force from abroad could or should be used against major
assaults on human rights, there was reason to applaud *The
Responsibility to Protect*. The document moved beyond the
Kosovo Report in defining a humanitarian right of intervention,
and with each step the definition became more elaborate. But
it remained no more than a well-intentioned declaration without any legal force, so generalized that attempts to apply it
could always be rejected by interested parties. Its influence
could only be proven in practice, and given the lamentable
record that marked the years after 1989 it could as easily be
dismissed for its naïveté or hypocrisy as praised for its far-

sighted humanity. Four years later, the UN General Assembly, in its *tour d'horizon* of all good causes in 2005, agreed to this pale statement of intention arising from the report:

> The international community, through the United Nations ... has the responsibility to use appropriate diplomatic, humanitarian and other peaceful means ... to help to protect populations from genocide, war crimes, ethnic cleansing and crimes against humanity. In this context we are prepared to take collective action, in a timely and decisive manner, through the Security Council, in accordance with the Charter, including Chapter VII, on a case-by-case basis and in cooperation with relevant regional organizations as appropriate, should peaceful means be inadequate and national authorities are manifestly failing to protect their populations ...[95]

The work of two international commissions over two years came down to this. Canadian Ambassador Allan Rock, who lobbied hard for the resolution, said "we take particular Canadian pride that the *Responsibility to Protect* has now been given express international global recognition and endorsement. It's been one of our priorities ... Now we're delighted that the leaders of the world will embrace it, so that we never again face another Rwanda."[96] Sudanese paramilitary assaults on the residents of Darfur province were then in their third year. In September 2004 they had been described by US Secretary of State Colin Powell as genocide. In the summer of 2006, international action to contain the violence remains fumbling and inadequate.

The American Empire Confronts the Barbarians

By the time of his next non-fiction book in 2003, Michael Ignatieff had moved from his freelance career in London to the directorship of the Carr Center for Human Rights Policy at Harvard University. The role of the centre is to train future public servants and conduct research, "guided by a commitment to make human rights principles central to the formulation of public policy in United States and throughout the world." As director, Ignatieff was centrally involved in a "Project on the Means of Intervention," which examined "how humanitarian considerations are factored into, and affected by, military intervention." The project brought active and retired US military and security specialists together with human rights and aid organizations, aiming "ultimately"—in the centre's words—to make "the use of military power more consistent with humanitarian principles."[97]

Like every resident of the United States in the autumn of 2001, Ignatieff observed and shared in the shock and political turmoil that engulfed the country after the suicide attacks on New York and Washington. The attacks transformed the moral and intellectual atmosphere of the United States. In January of that year, the new Republican administration of George W. Bush had taken office, and with it a coterie of neoconservative advisors in the White House and the Department of Defense whose views had been promoted in the pages of the *Weekly Standard*, the *Wall Street Journal*, the op-ed pages of the *New York Times*, *Commentary* magazine, the *National Review*, and the web site of the *Project for a New American Century*. They were both idealistic and self-consciously tough, the promoters of a proud, unapologetic, and aggressive America who believed that America's destiny was to manage the world in its own interest.[98] For the first eight months of the Bush presidency, their attitudes were not widely reflected in the policies of the new president, but after 9/11 he leaned heavily on them to guide him in a world where the United States seemed, for the first time in its history, to be under direct threat. In the mood of panic and disorientation that followed the September attacks, the press and public were ready to accept the same guidance. Criticism was smothered in a wave of nationalist fervour that revealed strong elements of suspicion and intolerance, and a demoralized Democratic Party abandoned its role as a critical opponent of the White House. It was difficult, in this stifling atmosphere, to maintain or express an independent perspective on the world—but it was not impossible.

During this time, Ignatieff remained a prolific journalist, writing frequently in the *New York Review of Books*, the *New York Times*, and the *Guardian*. Clearly, his thoughts had been evolving towards accepting a dominant role for American power well before September 11: the liberal internationalist of the 1990s had found the world an unaccommodating place. But the sudden change in America's mood had an added and profound effect on his perspectives. As he noted in the Preface to *Empire Lite: Nation-Building in Bosnia, Kosovo and Afghanistan*, he moved away, in these years, from reporting about ethnic war, collapsing states, and military intervention to considering "the imperial struggle to impose order once intervention has occurred."

He called this "the nation-building enterprise"—a phrase as deceptive as "humanitarian intervention" or "virtual war"—and recognized that it requires "temporary imperialism" or "empire lite" for its achievement.[99] The United States was its agent. Ignatieff did not sound skeptical of the new Bush administration.

He was already anxious about the dangers posed by Iraq. When the US air force used guided missiles to bomb an Iraqi radar control system just one month after Bush assumed office in January 2001 (which the president described as a "routine mission"), Ignatieff chastised Bush in the *New York Times* for underplaying the threat from Baghdad:

> ... it's not clear why the President keeps pretending that Saddam does not already possess weapons of mass destruction. Weeks before the February 16 strikes, reports appeared in the British press, based on information supplied by Iraqi defectors, that Saddam had two operational atomic bombs in his arsenal. The administration neither confirms nor denies these reports in public, but in recent testimony before the Senate Intelligence Committee, CIA director George Tenet conceded that since the Desert Fox air strikes of 1998, Iraq had rebuilt "key portions" of its chemical weapons capability. If the CIA is correct, the President is misleading the public: Saddam Hussein's weapons of mass destruction ... are already in his arsenal: deadly nerve agents like VX and sarin, biological agents like anthrax and botulin, together

with the missiles to deliver them against its neighbors, especially Israel and Iran.[100]

The UN's containment policy against Iraq, Ignatieff insisted, had failed in almost all its aspects, and American efforts to promote domestic revolt were inept. "Whatever we do, we do not seem close to eliminating Saddam's weapons of mass destruction." Ignatieff quoted the prominent Iraqi exile Kanan Makiya as saying that " 'What we need is a General MacArthur,' i.e., an American occupation of the entire country to create democracy from the bottom up." But Ignatieff conceded that "America has no stomach for 'nation-building,' " and concluded that there was no alternative to a long struggle of wills with Hussein, during which the United States should not risk "cut[ting] that struggle short." The message was ambiguous: Take note of Baghdad's dangerous weapons, tighten containment of Iraq, but think about that reference to General MacArthur.[101]

Three weeks after the September 11 attacks, Ignatieff offered his judgement on their nature. They were not political attacks, meant to achieve specific political goals. "What we are up against," he suggested, "is apocalyptic nihilism," intended to bring about a violent transformation of a corrupted world. Nothing can be done to appease the hatreds behind these deeds; there is nothing to be negotiated. "Since the politics of reason cannot defeat apocalyptic nihilism, we must fight. Force is legitimate to the degree that it is discriminate, and to the degree that it is discriminate, it is just."[102]

So there is bound to be war, and "a war against terror is bound to be a dirty war." Americans owe neither restraint nor mercy to the enemy, who has shown none. They owe such restraint only to themselves, to their own moral scruples. "The combatants who will wage this war in our name will have to live with what they do. To execute the innocent, to visit death on civilians, even to torture the guilty, would haunt those who serve in our name. For that reason alone, a war against terror must be discriminate, proportional and restrained."[103]

The British and the Spanish, he noted, have managed to live with terror while preserving democracy and the rule of law: They have lessons for the United States in keeping their security forces within constitutional control. The Americans begin this war, by contrast, with an unsavory record from their own "covert operations in foreign countries" during previous decades, which will tempt them to ignore civilized behaviour.

This was a salutary warning to show restraint, but it was flaccid, because it accompanied a call to arms against what was seen as a mysterious, unrestrained, unappeasable, unidentified enemy. A "war against terrorism" was something new that granted licence for excess by its very name. It was not war under the normal rules of war. It was even less a police operation, as the British and Spanish governments had officially treated their responses to domestic terrorist groups. In those instances, there had been only the most limited application of special laws.[104] Ignatieff accepted the language of "the war on terror" and continued to use the phrase as the consequences of doing so gradually revealed themselves. For the Bush administration, it was a brilliant (although dangerous) propaganda device and a constitutional escape into the use of emergency powers without limits of time or degree. For liberal democrats, it was equally a betrayal of limits and precision. And it was insincere. As the English philosopher Mary Midgley wrote, every great power had supported terrorists for its own purposes, and terrorists "do not compose a coherent nation that can be conquered."[105] The idea of a vague and permanent enemy seemed to be a leftover from the Cold War.

> In ordinary, literal wars, this suspending of normal human relations is supposed to be just a temporary expedient, made necessary by an emergency. Everybody views it as an evil, to be got rid of as soon as the situation allows. The corrupt thing about the Cold War idea was that it legitimised acceptance of this evil as a normal, permanent condition of life. It domesticated tribal hatred.
>
> It seems to me that this habit is what has made it possible for us to drift into the muddled idea of a 'war' which is (on the one hand) a literal war, fought with actual bombs, but it is also (on the other) a kind of endless, chronic, ideal conflict against an abstraction as cloudy as terrorism, a conflict which can never be won.[106]

Terrorism can only be conquered politically, or surrendered to, which is what Ignatieff began his reflections by denying. (The settlements with the IRA in Northern Ireland and ETA in Spain are two recent examples of such successful political achievement.)

By the end of 2001, Ignatieff was writing as an American. There were probably complex reasons for this: his lifelong admiration for the American myth; the fact that he had moved from the United Kingdom to his new academic post at Harvard; his experiences of the previous ten years, which had led him more and more to favour the expansive use of American power in the world; the brutal and unifying influences of September 11; and, as the writer Andrew Potter pointed out in 2006, the need to attune himself to his audience because public intellectuals need an audience. "When you read all that Ignatieff has written since 9/11," Potter writes, "it is clear that he has been writing as a centre-left Canadian trying to find the pitch of American public discourse."[107] And American public discourse had moved sharply to the right.

In two reviews published almost simultaneously in the *New York Times* and the *New York Review of Books* in February 2002, Ignatieff compared contemporary America to the Roman Empire under barbarian threat.[108] The Roman parallel struck him forcibly: "America has now felt the tremor of dread that the ancient world must have known when Rome was first sacked. Then and now an imperial people has come awake to the menace of the barbarians ... Retribution has been visited on the barbarians [in Afghanistan], and more will follow, but the American military knows it has begun a campaign without an obvious end in sight. The most carefree and confident empire in history now grimly confronts the question of whether it can escape Rome's ultimate fate."[109]

Ignatieff had chosen his role as chronicler and advocate of the American empire. He lamented that, after the end of the Cold War in 1991, Washington believed it could dominate the world without pain. But the distant fringes of empire were falling into chaos, and chaos had now reached the homeland. The giant had been roused from its slumber, and it would act—alone when it wished, with others when it must. (The others would provide policing and humanitarian aid in the border zones.) Ignatieff acknowledged that this was a different world from the cooperative one imagined by "liberal international lawyers and human rights activists." The new world order was being shaped to serve American imperial goals, and America would ignore or sabotage those international bodies that failed to serve its interests. This was a fact. But Ignatieff rejected the realist view of American writer Robert Kaplan that the United States should avoid humanitarian intervention or the efforts of nation-building abroad. This was "tragic pessimism" or "gloomy fatalism," and its effect would be baleful if Washington heeded Kaplan's advice. In Ignatieff's world, there was a nation to be built in Afghanistan—and others over the horizon. That job would have to be done under American direction.[110]

The tremors from 9/11 rolled on. In the same month, Ignatieff worried in the *New York Times* that the era of human rights was over. Bush's war on terror had displaced human rights from the list of America's official concerns, and silenced other nations as they enlisted in America's war. Moscow identified its Chechen campaign as part of the war on terror, and the crimes of all the regimes needing American support could now be excused as they enlisted in the cause. The climate, Ignatieff said, recalled that of the Cold War. He pleaded weakly that human rights advocates should not give up their work, but should work more quietly under repressive regimes to help create political stability.[111]

For a few months, he tried awkwardly to straddle the abyss between the international human rights movement and the new American campaign against terrorism. But the abyss was widening. Ignatieff's convictions about the need for American dominance inclined him increasingly to the side of the Bush administration. In March 2002, he argued in *The Chronicle of Higher Education* that the international debate on human rights was itself a product of American hegemony: "We would not have a global ascendancy of human rights and a global language of freedom ... without the ascendancy of the American empire. I don't care how controversial it is to say so."[112] The article's author noted that Ignatieff's move to Harvard coincided with "his growing influence on global-policy thinking."

> This path was perhaps prefigured in a line from a Judy Garland song that his mother used to sing to him: "People say don't stop—unless you've played the Palace, you haven't played the top." Playing the Palace, Mr. Ignatieff says, meant playing the United States or Britain.
>
> He played the British Palace for 20 years. His performance at the American one is just getting underway. The crowd is gathering and listening intently.[113]

"I temperamentally think better on the road," Ignatieff remarked to the same reporter, "with my laptop jouncing around, and I haven't had enough sleep."[114] He hadn't been in Kabul for six years, and in the early summer of 2002 he took off from Harvard to see how nation-building was coming along in Afghanistan after the expulsion of the Taliban. The jaunt gave him a fresh opportunity to use his talent for vivid description on the frontiers between order and disorder. He reflected on his experiences in an essay for the *New York Times Magazine* called "Nation-Building Lite," in July 2002.[115]

In Mazar-i-Sharif, Ignatieff visited the compound of a local warlord where he met a "bulky American in combat camouflage, sleeveless pocket vest, wraparound sunglasses and floppy fishing hat" who refused to talk to him. Surrounded by armed mujahedeen, "the heavyset American is the one who matters." Ignatieff had shifted with the winds of 9/11, moving away from rescuing failed states to defending the world from terrorism. He talked now about American interests, not about human rights, and he talked tough to his American readers.

> Call it peace-keeping or nation-building, call it what you like—imperial policing is what is going on in Mazar. In fact, America's entire war on terror is an exercise in imperialism …
>
> These garrisons are by no means temporary. Terror can't be controlled unless order is built in the anarchic zones where terrorists find shelter. In Afghanistan, this means nation-building, creating a state strong enough to keep Al Qaeda from returning. But the Bush administration wants to do this on the cheap, at the lowest level of investment and risk. In Washington they call this nation-building lite. But empires don't come lite. They come heavy, or they do not last. And neither does the peace they are meant to preserve.[116]

The Americans were too thin on the ground, because "the Bush administration needs all the legions at its disposal for a potential operation against Iraq." (The word had been out since the president's "axis of evil" declaration in January 2002, and the signs of preparation were multiplying in Washington and London.) To disarm the Afghan warlords, create a national army, police the country, raise revenues, and establish order would take years, if it could be done at all. But Ignatieff was now setting his sights low. The most he hoped for was "... ordered anarchy, among loosely controlled regional fiefs ... This may be all that is possible, and it may be all that American interests require. Keeping expectations realistic is the key to staying the course here. Understanding what's at stake is just as important. America could still lose here. If it did, Al Qaeda would secure a victory as large as it achieved on 9/11."[117]

What Ignatieff saw around him was a vast imperial confusion of American forces, competing Afghani factions, UN managers, NGOs running relief and reconstruction projects, a flourishing drug economy, and an impoverished population. After the descriptions of disorder, he returned to his preaching: "The empire wants quick results, and that means an early exit. The Afghans want us to protect them, and at the same time help them back on their feet. That means sticking around for a while. Washington had better decide what it wants ..."[118]

This comment was both a warning and passionate appeal to the American public and the Bush administration: nation-building is necessary, but "nation-building lite" will not be enough. Ignatieff desperately wanted the American mission to succeed by doing more. And at its core, he knew, that mission was military. But the military would have to depend on the Afghans themselves. He closed the article with two paragraphs of soap-opera bathos about a woman teaching young girls to read in an open-air school, and a brick-maker with his five-year-old son, making bricks of straw and mud in the dwindling twilight. The Americans in floppy hats were there to keep them safe.

Months before this visit to Afghanistan, charges of American mistreatment of prisoners taken in the Afghan War had made headlines in the United States and abroad. American television audiences saw pictures of blindfolded prisoners shoved into and enclosed in metal shipping containers. Canadians discussed pictures of Afghans captured by Canadian special forces and transferred to the Americans. President Bush's designation of prisoners as "unlawful combatants" who would not benefit from the protections of the Geneva Conventions was the object of continuous protest from human rights organizations. By the spring of 2002, the American dispatch of hundreds of prisoners to a makeshift camp at Guantánamo Bay, Cuba, for detention without charge and beyond the jurisdiction of American courts, was a subject of international scandal. Within the United States, the Patriot Act had diminished American freedoms, and thousands of Muslim students from the Middle East had been arrested and deported from the country. But the analyst of human rights policy did not investigate nor did he write any articles of complaint.

As the American liberal left began to splinter over humanitarian intervention, over Kosovo, and above all over the appropriate response to September 11, Ignatieff was bound to become a target of criticism from his former associates. One of them was the American writer David Rieff. Rieff was a counterpart to Ignatieff: born in the same generation, the son of distinguished parents, educated at Princeton, an editor and public intellectual, a reporter on the ground during the Yugoslav Wars, a supporter of the Kosovo and Afghan Wars and, like Ignatieff, "an intellectual who's willing to get shot at." But he contrasted himself to Ignatieff in seeing himself only as a critic: "… whatever authority I've earned is that I really am not simultaneously trying to get a job."[119]

In his book *A Bed for the Night: Humanitarianism in Crisis* (2002), Rieff recalled that the humanitarian movement flowered in the 1990s as a secular religion when Western states left relief to the private agencies in the collapsing states of southeastern Europe, and then refused to intervene because that would endanger the life-saving. But in Kosovo, the opposite occurred. The great powers were tired of Milosevic's troublemaking, so they claimed a humanitarian crisis as a pretext for intervention. But there was no humanitarian crisis, only serious violations of rights that did not justify war. Nevertheless humanitarians accepted the war. The human crisis came after the NATO attack, not before. "So increasingly, there was a kind of historic compromise, a kind of marriage, a kind of fusion between humanitarianism, which started as an independent, impartial, separate idea, with state power. Now, after Kosovo and Afghanistan, and now with this looming war in Iraq, it's harder and harder to see where the space is between the great powers' interest and the humanitarian enterprise."[120] Once the aid movements joined themselves to the power of the state, they lost their independent leverage against it and became its agents. Rieff criticized Ignatieff for supporting the alliance of American imperial power with humanitarian aid, for exaggerating what armed interventions could actually achieve, and for raising utopian hopes among suffering peoples that could not be realized. "We have seen that such hopes—in the UN, in 'the international community'—were misguided, at times even suicidal."[121]

Ignatieff responded to Rieff in an unusually severe review of the book in December 2002, accusing Rieff of inconsistency and wrongheadedness. The real challenge in places like Bosnia, Kosovo, and Afghanistan, Ignatieff insisted, was not to decry military intervention, but "to understand that there are moments when one must choose a lesser evil in order to avoid a greater one. The greater evil in Bosnia was to sit back and watch the Serbs cleanse their way to a greater Serbia. In Kosovo the greater evil would have been to watch Milosevic proceed to crush the Kosovar people. In Afghanistan it would have been to stand by while the country was used by Al-Qaeda as a base for international terrorism. If you want to avoid those evils, humanitarian action will not be enough. You will have to take military action."[122]

Ignatieff's book *Empire Lite* was published in the spring of 2003 as the Iraq War was beginning. The first three chapters reprint previously published essays, while the last one reflects on the nature of the new American empire and the ambiguous situation of human rights in the imperial territories. Bosnia, Kosovo, and Afghanistan are all imperial outposts, Ignatieff explained, because their stability is necessary to the security of the major powers and requires the presence of foreign armies and because all three are effectively governed from abroad. They are only under official United Nations protection—while many other failed states are not—because the United States decided that was practical and appropriate. In both Bosnia and Kosovo, American self-interest was conveniently allied with "the language of human rights." In Afghanistan, American security was paramount, while any gains for human rights came as bonuses, not as reasons for the war.

The empire is not consistent in its defence of human rights, Ignatieff said, because that would commit American armies to every corner of the world. Instead, "empires that are successful learn to ration their services to moral principle to the few strategic zones where the defence of principle is simultaneously the defence of a vital interest, and where the risks do not outweigh the benefits. This is why modern imperial ethics can only be hypocritical."[123] The American empire will never confront the Russians or the Chinese over human rights because the risks are too great, but this does not mean that the claim to value human rights everywhere is false.

The empire, he notes, does not consist solely of Americans—it has useful Japanese and European "paymasters"—but it depends on American leadership, and "its moral grace notes are all liberal and democratic. Its purpose is to extend free elections, rule of law, democratic self-government to peoples who have only known fratricide."[124] But democracy and imperial rule are contradictory, so the troops and viceroys set exit timetables in advance: "… if you behave, you will be masters in your own house; if you don't, we will abandon you to your warlords."[125] Ignatieff reminds his readers that this kind of pattern has existed before: in the British Empire after the mid-nineteenth century, when self-governing colonies moved slowly towards independence, and in Palestine after 1919, when Britain was mandated to lead Arabs and Jews to "some kind of self-government." The contrast today is that the timetable is so short. The new imperialists lack patience.

Ignatieff attributes this impatience to the electoral politics of Western democracies. They work to a domestic electoral cycle, and politicians do not want to face imperial troubles during election years: "… it takes a determined exercise of leadership to convince people that expenditure on nation-building is necessary for their security."[126] (Ignatieff weights the scales of judgement here by calling what the American troops and their allies are doing "nation-building.")

Ignatieff admits that—beyond democratic impatience— there is one historical experience that hinders America's imperial adventures. The ghost of Vietnam still haunts America: for the United States, it was "an imperial nation-building project, an attempt to use military power to sustain a democratic republic ..." (if South Vietnam in the 1960s could be called that). But the imperial power faced a domestic nation-building project on the part of the Viet Cong, and the experience of Vietnam shows "that nationalism will always prove to be the nemesis of any imperial nation-building project."[127] On the other hand, since Vietnam there have been many, mostly failed domestic nation-building projects elsewhere. These are the ones, Ignatieff proposes, "for which temporary empire remains a solution."[128]

Afghanistan, he admits, is a special case. Here, in the 1990s, the West tolerated the Pakistani intelligence service's support for the Taliban as nation-builders. They gained power; Al Qaeda came to stay and took control of the state; and "the empire had to beat the barbarians back and start nation-building all over again."[129] But he warns that Afghanistan is a tough nation which has cast off imperial intruders from Britain and Russia before and could easily do so again.

Ignatieff reminds us that contemporary belief in human equality and national self-determination is the result of the liberal anti-colonial campaigns of the last seventy years, but somehow the effort to achieve them has failed.

It is at least ironic that liberal believers in
these ideas—someone like me, for example —
can end up supporting the creation of a new
humanitarian empire, a new form of colonial
tutelage for the peoples of Kosovo, Bosnia
and Afghanistan. The reason simply is that,
however right these principles may be, the
political form in which they are realized—the
nationalist nation-building project—so often
fails to deliver them. For every nationalist
struggle that succeeds in giving its people
self-determination and dignity, there are
more that only deliver their people up to a
self-immolating slaughter, terror, enforced
partition and failure.[130]

History has not worked as liberals hoped it would. "The
age of empire ought to have been succeeded by an age of
independent, equal and self-governing nation states. In reality it has been succeeded by an age of ethnic cleansing and
state failure."[131] And so empire has returned to make
another try. (It could also be—one might add—that the
modern world was always more complex and mysterious
than the Western liberal mind could comprehend.)

Empire Lite concludes with another secular sermon. It is
bleak. First the blame: for thirty years after Vietnam, the
Western world ignored the growing collapse of order in the
borderlands, placing its faith in development, and then in
globalization, neither of which can work without safe streets,
schools, and hospitals. Dictatorships can provide those goods,
but only democracies accepting the rule of law are likely to be
"stable, secure and at peace with their neighbours."

Then the challenge: "Nothing less than the reconstruction of a global order of stable nations is required."

Then the prospect: "[T]emporary imperial rule" will have to "provide the force and will necessary to bring order out of chaos."[132] But American imperial power cannot meet the demand for its services, so most societies will have to "create themselves, and the instrument they commonly use to do so is war."

> In the end there cannot be order in the world, and certainly no justice, without democratic self-rule. Every people need not have a state, but people must rule themselves. But to reach that destination, the peoples who do not rule themselves will have to struggle, and while empire can help, repress and contain the struggle, it cannot control it.[133]

In Bosnia, Kosovo, and Afghanistan the empire must force responsibility onto local elites while preventing foreign invasion or civil war. Ignatieff claims that is not what it is doing. Instead, he repeats his complaint that America still tries to do everything "on the cheap, from day to day, without the long-term security guarantees and short-term financial assistance that would genuinely create the conditions for true national independence." This approach risks losing everything, "since peoples disillusioned with our promises will have enduring reasons never to trust us again."[134]

Ignatieff's Utopian Vision

The outlook for the world may indeed be bleak, but that concluding appeal in *Empire Lite* for a more resolute America just as it entered an unnecessary war of its own choice in Iraq was ominous. And it was also misguided.

Ignatieff's distant vision on the far horizon—of order, justice, and democratic self-rule for all—is a utopian goal that is so far beyond human hope that the expectation of it is bound to be dashed in endless impossible ventures. It is a vision that matches the Marxist (or the Christian) promised land in its grandiosity. Lost along with it will be many more modest goals that are achievable, if they are not caught up in the train of such majestic and destructive fantasy.

There is, as well, Ignatieff's prophetic arrogance: for how has he gained the insight to know that the world, as he tells us in passing, "is experiencing what Europe lived through in the Hundred Years War"?[135] (Counting from the close of the Cold War in 1989, one hundred years of war would take us to 2089, unless history passes more quickly in the twenty-first century.)

And there is, finally, Ignatieff's failure to face the immediate reality, on a smaller but still atrocious scale, of an imminent new American war that was never intended by its promoters in the White House and the defense department to be a humanitarian venture. (Yet he speaks of a "humanitarian empire" that is about to launch the war.) The winter of 2003 was a time for Ignatieff to pay closer attention to the evidence around him, of what his imaginary America was really doing to itself and to the world. It was a time to listen carefully to the words and observe the acts of Bush and Donald Rumsfeld, rather than dreaming that they were about to perform another work of liberation in Iraq.

CHAPTER 3

Iraq and Lesser Evils

By the end of 2001, the United States and the Afghan Northern Alliance had driven the Taliban from power in Afghanistan, and Al Qaeda had retreated to its mountain hideaways on the Afghan-Pakistan border. A pro-American regime had been installed in Kabul that hoped eventually to establish its legitimate authority throughout the country, a UN blessing had been conferred, and the international aid agencies had begun to pour their resources into the liberated capital city. Osama bin Laden had escaped, but the Bush administration nevertheless congratulated itself on a deceptively easy victory in its war against terror. Without pause, the White House and the Pentagon began planning for a larger war.

Vice President Richard B. Cheney and others in Washington had made known their desire to remove President Hussein from power during President Bush's first term. Until September 11, they lacked any pretext for war: the suicide attacks on the United States would provide it. Hussein had been no friend of Al Qaeda or fundamentalist Islam, and there was no evidence, immediate or remote, of Iraq's association with the terrorist network. Bush ordered his intelligence advisors to find it. At the end of January 2002, the president, who had already declared himself to be a war president, labelled his global opponents the "axis of evil." There were three of them: Iraq, Syria, and North Korea. But it was clear that the list was stitched together to give Bush dramatic cover to hunt down the defiant autocrat who had survived expulsion from Kuwait a decade before. Hussein was in Washington's gunsights. For a year, what followed was housekeeping. "The intelligence and facts were being fixed around the policy," the Director of Britain's Secret Intelligence Service, Sir Richard Dearlove, told a meeting in Prime Minister Blair's office on July 23, 2002, after returning from high level briefings in Washington. "There was a perceptible shift in attitude," he reported. "Military action was now seen as inevitable. Bush wanted to remove Saddam, through military action, justified by the conjunction of terrorism and WMD [weapons of mass destruction] … The NSC [National Security Council] had no patience with the UN route …There was little discussion in Washington of the aftermath after military action."[136] Britain's support for war had apparently been sealed in an agreement between Bush and Blair at a meeting in April.[137] By the spring of 2002, American forces were being scaled down in Afghanistan to begin a buildup of units preparing for the assault on Iraq.

While the signs of an impending war multiplied through the summer of 2002, Ignatieff published nothing on the subject. In June, President Bush told graduates at West Point that his government was preparing a new strategic doctrine that would declare America's right to engage in pre-emptive military action against any state that it judged to be hostile, and in September the White House published the National Security Strategy confirming that policy.[138] It was the doctrinal justification for war, resting on the foun-

dations of American righteousness, dominant power, and
self-interest. From August onwards, there were increasingly
dire warnings from senior members of the US administration—especially Vice President Cheney, Defense Secretary
Rumsfeld, and Rumsfeld's associate Paul Wolfowitz—asserting that Iraq was rapidly building its stockpiles of weapons
of mass destruction, which constituted a clear and present
danger to the security of the United States. In September,
the Blair government published an alarmist "dossier" on
Britain's imminent danger, asserting that Iraq possessed
biological and chemical warheads for medium-range
missiles that could be armed and launched within forty-five
minutes of an order to use them. In October, Condoleezza
Rice told a television interviewer, "We don't want the smok-
ing gun to be a mushroom cloud." All these warnings took
the form of statements of fact, offered without equivocation.
"The campaign of persuasion," wrote the *New Yorker's*
George Packer, "proceeded by rhetorical hyperbole, by the
deliberate slanting of ambiguous facts in one direction, and
by a wink-and-nod suggestion that the administration knew
more than it could reveal."[139]

Shortly before publication of the British dossier, Prime
Minister Blair convinced President Bush that they should seek
the return of United Nations arms inspectors to Iraq and ask
for UN Security Council approval before any pre-emptive
attack. In October, the renewed inspections began, and for
five months the political charade was played out in New York
and Baghdad while Washington insisted that its actions in
Iraq would not be restrained by the Security Council.
Simultaneously the US Senate and Congress, acting after
urgent briefing from the White House and the intelligence
agencies, adopted a joint resolution authorizing the president

"to use the Armed Forces of the United States as he determines to be necessary and appropriate in order to defend the national security of the United States against the continuing threat posed by Iraq ..."[140] The resolution was opposed by about a quarter of the members of both houses—most of them Democrats. This was Bush's Gulf of Tonkin resolution, produced in a carefully promoted atmosphere of fear.

Throughout these months of preparation for war, there were frequent articles in the *Washington Post*, the *Los Angeles Times*, the *Guardian*, the *Independent*, the *Nation*, and elsewhere raising doubts about the honesty and reliability of the case for war being made by the Bush and Blair governments.[141]

The silence of Michael Ignatieff throughout this period of controversy and the inexorable countdown to war seems remarkable. What can explain it? In October 2001, in the midst of the Afghan campaign, he commented in the *Guardian* on "what we are fighting for, and what victory would look like if it is achieved."[142] He was not talking about Afghanistan, but about "President George Bush's call to arms—bring the evil-doers to justice or bring justice to the evil-doers." He was taking the long view. Victory in the Second World War, he recalled, was not achieved until the 1950s, "when a democratic Germany and Japan emerged from occupation." In this new war against Osama bin Laden, there would not be a military victory, but only a slow process of weaning support away from bin Laden on the Arab streets, and that would require a just settlement of the Israeli-Palestinian conflict, dictated and enforced by "western states."[143] Beyond that, there was "a global world order" to be reconstructed by the victors of the Cold War: failed states to be rebuilt, foreign aid budgets to be enlarged,

Third World debt to be overcome, the AIDS epidemic to be halted. This agenda was an ambitious one. While it did not mention more humanitarian wars, it also did not exclude them. Indeed, they were required. "Bringing justice to the evil-doers," in Ignatieff's definition, must have been what he meant a few months later when he wrote in *Empire Lite* of the Hundred Years War. But he did not utter the name of Iraq. Perhaps the next step on this long journey had not yet come into focus for him, although it was doing so quickly for the White House. Bush was going to war.

Part of the explanation for Ignatieff's silence may be that he is not a political reporter, a historian of war, or even a practised political analyst. He is an impressionistic writer, a cultural critic, a human rights activist, an ethicist. Out in the field, he can draw compelling word pictures of men and women in distress; he can make persuasive appeals for their relief, but he seldom offers any detailed explanation of the politics that put them into that distress or of what will, realistically, get them out of it, if anything can. He prefers writing about painful events, either on the scene or on a grand historical scale. Don't bother, he seems to say, about the complex interplay of the politicians working behind the scenes; don't bother to ask what those politicians think they are doing; don't bother about their motives; don't bother about the evidence; don't bother about trying to anticipate unexpected results; don't bother to learn why things happened the way they did. But historical truth is usually in the details, and understanding fails without them.

After 9/11, in any case, all that was probably irrelevant for Ignatieff. He seemed to have decided that the saviour of the world in this century would have to be the

American empire. The details might be troublesome. He had chosen to be a promoter of the empire in its long-term conflict with the barbarians. Raising his sights to that level was, perhaps, one way of escaping from the realities of the present. In the summer of 2006, he said that making any criticism of the dubious claims of the Bush administration about Iraq's weapons of mass destruction before the Iraq War would have been "misplaced specificity." The important thing was to remove Hussein from power, and not to undermine the American and British case for war.[144]

As the propaganda campaign in favour of war in Iraq developed during 2002, Ignatieff remembered his visits to Iraqi Kurdistan a decade earlier, and the sickening evidence he had seen of Hussein's gas attacks on villages in 1988. He had read the powerful accounts of life under the tyrant in the writings of Kanan Makiya, and discussed Iraq with him. Makiya was Ignatieff's next-door neighbour in Cambridge, Massachusetts, and Ignatieff said that Makiya had "a very direct impact on me" in favour of war. Like Makiya, he could look beyond those horrors to an Iraq transformed by a humanitarian invasion. (In a meeting with President Bush and Vice President Cheney in January 2003, Makiya said that "People will greet the troops with sweets and flowers," a claim that Cheney made much of in his public statements before the war.)[145] Bush had begun to call that transformation by a different name: "regime change," which sounded suitably anodyne for his purposes. Given Ignatieff's own beliefs, it was not surprising that he would find this talk persuasive. But Bush and Ignatieff were speaking different languages.

In December 2002, George Packer talked with Ignatieff as one of those liberal hawks "who have done the most thinking and writing about how American power can be turned to good ends as well as bad, who don't see human rights and democracy as idealistic delusions, and who are struggling to figure out Iraq." A potential anti-war movement would need their intelligent support, but President Bush also needed them "to give a voice to his war aims, which he has largely kept to himself." Before coming down on one side or the other, they would have to settle their own divided minds. Ignatieff told Packer that " 'this one's really difficult … I am having real trouble with this because it's not clear to me that containment has failed.' " The moral struggle was one between fear and wish: fear warned that an invasion of Iraq would increase disorder both inside and outside the country, while wish promised that Iraq would be liberated from tyranny and the germ of democracy would be planted in the Middle East. To give way to fear, Ignatieff thought, would mean missing " 'a huge prize at the end.' " For Packer, "wish makes a liberal hawk sound like a Bush hawk, blithely unconcerned about the dangers of American power … This dilemma is every liberal's current dilemma."[146]

Ignatieff was about to make his choice. On January 5, 2003, his major article, "The Burden," was the cover feature in the *New York Times Magazine*.[147] As America's most influential newspaper, the *Times* was a notably uncritical supporter of President Bush's preparations for war against Iraq. There was no more privileged forum for Ignatieff to reveal his judgements on the coming war, or to affect the balance of popular opinion.

"The Burden" contained lengthy passages about the trials of empire from his book *Empire Lite*, which was due to appear within a few months, but the essay was freshly shaped around the implications of going to war in Iraq. Ignatieff set out to convince his readers with his romantic, mellifluous, slightly purple prose that America is, inescapably, an empire, and that an empire has high responsibilities.

> ... what word but "empire" describes the awesome thing that America is becoming? It is the only nation that polices the world through five global military commands; maintains more than a million men and women at arms on four continents; deploys carrier battle groups on watch in every ocean; guarantees the survival of countries from Israel to ... South Korea; drives the wheels of global trade and commerce; and fills the hearts and minds of an entire planet with its dreams and desires.

Being an imperial power, he said, meant setting the world's rules. (If there is any note of irony in this assertion, it is deeply hidden.)

> It means enforcing such order as there is in the world and doing so in the American interest. It means laying down the rules America wants (on everything from markets to weapons of mass destruction) while exempting itself from other rules (the Kyoto Protocol on climate change and the International Criminal Court) that go against its interest. It also means carrying out imperial functions in places America has inherited from the failed empires of the 20th century—

> Ottoman, British and Soviet. In the 21st
> century, America rules alone, struggling to
> manage the insurgent zones ... that have
> proved to be the nemeses of empires past.

Iraq demonstrated what the imperial role now involved.
The state was "an imperial fiction" created at Versailles in
1919, always held together by force, and now terrorized by
"an expansionist rights violator." The United Nations had
ignored him "until an American president seized it by the
scruff of the neck and made it bark. Multilateral solutions to
the world's problems are all very well, but they have no
teeth unless America bares its fangs."

Ignatieff noted that the new National Security Strategy
pledged that America would lead the world towards free
markets and liberal democracy. The Strategy was cast in
the redemptive language of Woodrow Wilson, and what it
meant in Iraq was that the United States would commit
itself "to become the guarantor of peace, stability, democ-
ratization and oil supplies in a combustible region of
Islamic peoples stretching from Egypt to Afghanistan."
Would this mean, he wondered, that "in becoming an
empire it risks losing its soul as a republic"? Would the
imperial power overextend itself abroad, abandon its civic
and egalitarian goals at home and destroy its own liberties?
Every empire eventually faced nemesis, and now America
had to confront "a remote possibility that seems to haunt
the history of empire: hubris followed by defeat." But
American readers could take heart: Pride and defeat were
only "a remote possibility."

Now the imperial course was set: it was too late for
America to turn back even if it wished to do so. Since

September 11, the United States could only be safe at home by policing abroad. "Iraq represents the first in a series of struggles to contain the proliferation of weapons of mass destruction, the first attempt to shut off the potential supply of lethal technologies to a global terrorist network." The White House's conclusion that containment would no longer work "is not unreasonable." Waiting would only increase the danger that Hussein would become master of the entire region and manipulator of the world's energy supplies. Years of sanctions had punished the Iraqi people, rather than the regime, and UN weapons inspections could easily be evaded. "That leaves us, but only as a reluctant last resort, with regime change."

Here Ignatieff had a few admonitory words for "left wingers and right-wing isolationists" : Vietnam might have brought defeat and disgrace, but other American imperial ventures had brought freedom to the Japanese, the Germans, the Bosnians, the Kosovars. "The list of people whose freedom depends on American air and ground power also includes the Afghans and, most inconveniently of all, the Iraqis." For human rights groups dismayed by the prospect of a British and American invasion, Ignatieff offered not reasoning but rebuke: "The disagreeable reality for those who believe in human rights is that there are some occasions—and Iraq may be one of them—when war is the only real remedy for regimes that live by terror."[148]

By entering Iraq, Ignatieff warned, the United States was taking on "the reordering of the entire region" on a long timetable. Bringing order to Iraq alone would take a decade. Iran would have to be reassured that it was not threatened by an Iraqi democracy next door; the Syrians would have to be nudged into peacemaking with Israel; the Saudis would have to be "coaxed" to become democrats; and above all, the United States would have to impose and enforce a just peace on Israel and Palestine. Without the creation of a stable and viable Palestinian state, America and Israel could never free themselves from the continuing threat of terrorism. This whole, daunting program was what made an Iraq invasion "an imperial act": to achieve a sustainable peace, Bush would have to set this entire revolution in motion, and his successors would have to see it through. "Again," Ignatieff counselled, "the paradox of the Iraqi operation is that half measures are more dangerous than whole measures. Imperial powers do not have the luxury of timidity, for timidity is not prudence, it is a confession of weakness. The question, then, is not whether America is too powerful but whether it is powerful enough. Does it have what it takes to be grandmaster of what Colin Powell has called the chessboard of the world's most inflammable region?"

While he urged Americans to accept this enlarged vision of their country's destiny, the writer repeated his warnings that pride and military overextension could bring the empire down. And to add another complication, he concluded that the United States would have little influence on the outcome, since the current crisis was essentially an internal civil war between fanatics and reactionaries within the Islamic world. The message seemed self-contradictory, but what could be distilled from it in Washington was that this liberal internationalist approved a war in Iraq as the first step of a great imperial adventure.

The essay offered no skepticism about President Bush's war based on evidence (already emerging) of its inadequate preparation; no questions about US intelligence being shaped by predetermined policy; no doubts about the claims of Iraqi links with Al Qaeda or the quality of Iraq's arsenals; no suggestion that renewed UN arms inspections needed time and might be effective: only urgings that Bush should enlarge his ambitions and act with overwhelming force and conviction. All these details passed below the line of Ignatieff's abstract and elevated vision. This was not analysis but cheerleading. "One didn't need special expertise in the fields of intelligence or proliferation to smell something wrong," Packer wrote later about this period in his fine study of the Iraq War, *The Assassins' Gate*.[149] If Ignatieff smelled something wrong, he neglected to tell his readers.

Despite the author's caution about the dangers of imperial overreach and hubris, "The Burden" was a stirring appeal to the American administration and public to don their armour of righteousness as they went into battle. That was the best gift that Ignatieff could give to the White House and the Pentagon in January 2003. It would cost Bush and Rumsfeld nothing to assure the skeptics that they would rise nobly to the occasion (although they would not call it imperial).

The war foretold was approaching week by week. As its opponents prepared their massive marches in London, Washington, Paris, Montreal, Rome, Madrid, and elsewhere, Secretary of State Powell made his tape-and-slide-show presentation to the UN Security Council, cataloguing the Bush government's evidence for Iraq's lethal arsenals of chemical, biological, and (soon to be) atomic weapons along with their rocket delivery systems. "These are not assertions. These are facts, corroborated by many sources, among them sources of the intelligence services of other countries," Powell told the world. Iraq had repeatedly withheld information, lied to the inspectors, failed its tests, he said. It could not be trusted. It had masses of weapons materials unaccounted for; it had mobile factories hidden in trucks and railway cars; it had aluminum tubes for processing enriched uranium; it had illegal missiles; it had unmanned aircraft; it had links with Al Qaeda; it had a murderous leader. "We must not shrink from whatever is ahead of us," he concluded. "We must not fail in our duty and our responsibility to the citizens of the countries that are represented in this body."[150]

The weapons inspectors were directed to continue their work in Iraq for a few more weeks, while Britain and the United States lobbied hard for a second Security Council resolution that would authorize the use of force against Iraq. The European community splintered over Anglo-American appeals for support, and Rumsfeld derided "old Europe" for its opposition to war. When the effort to gain a majority at the Security Council failed and the weapons inspectors reported their work incomplete, the United States and Britain withdrew their draft resolution, issued a short ultimatum, and attacked Iraq by air and land. Blair told the House of Commons that Britain, America, and their allies should act "with a clear conscience and a strong heart." On his part, he insisted, "I have never put our justification for action as regime change." He sought no more than Iraq's surrender of its weapons of mass destruction.[151]

Ignatieff explained his personal position in articles published in the *New York Times* and the *Guardian* within days of the invasion. Their main message was defensive: don't judge me by the company I keep. I don't like them. Bush's domestic policies were objectionable; "so-called unlawful combatants" shouldn't be locked up in Guantánamo and in military prisons without due process; the attorney general shouldn't be cavalier about civil rights;

the president shouldn't have bullied the Security Council. "But I still think the president is right when he says that Iraq and the world will be better off with Saddam disarmed, even, if necessary, through force."[152]

That issue was not the real one, he said. Everyone agreed that the world would be better after Saddam's removal. The real issue was "whether it is prudent to do so, whether the risks are worth running." The question was not moral but prudential, and Ignatieff admitted that the prudential costs were high.

> Who wants to live in a world where there are no stable rules for the use of force by states? Not me. Who wants to live in a world ruled by the military power of the strong? Not me. How will we oblige American military hegemony to pay "decent respect to the opinions of mankind"? I don't know. When the smoke of battle lifts, those who support the war will survey a battle zone that will include the ruins of the multilateral political order created in 1945.[153]

The risks, he said, could not be estimated. Was it worth improving the lives of twenty-five million people by killing some of them? Only, he thought, "if the gains in human freedom are large and the human costs are low. But let's admit it, the risks are large: the war may be bloody, the peace may be chaotic and what might be good in the long run for Iraqis might not be so good for Americans." The anger of the Muslim world towards America might also increase. "So what do we do? Isaiah

Berlin used to say that we just have to 'plump' for one option or the other in the absence of moral certainty or perfect knowledge of the future. We should also try to decide for ourselves, regardless of the company we keep, and that may include our friends, our family and our loved ones." Finally, he threw a parting grenade. "In the weeks and years ahead," he said, "the choices ... are about what risks are worth running when our safety depends on the answer. The real choices are going to be tougher than most of us could have ever imagined."[154]

A challenge was being thrown to his readers, then: Did he mean that if you don't agree with him on Iraq, you'll have to make harder choices and take even more risks with other peoples' lives when "the real choices" arrive? Or did he mean anything at all, beyond expressing his immediate moral confusion?

For two weeks the bombing attacks on Baghdad were relentless, and the advances of the US and British armies were swift. After sporadic firefights, the Iraqi army faded away and the leadership disappeared. By April 9 the iconic statue of Hussein on Freedom Square in Baghdad had been toppled, and on May 1 Bush announced from the flight deck of the aircraft carrier *Abraham Lincoln* that the mission in Iraq had been accomplished. The looting and violence in Baghdad had begun. Through the spring and summer, as the Coalition Provisional Authority stumbled over its shifting policies of pacification, disorder in the country grew steadily in scale. United Nations officials arrived to assist in reconstruction, but at the end of August their director was killed and their headquarters destroyed in a suicide bombing which led to withdrawal of the mission.

Taking His Distance

In September, Ignatieff offered his considered thoughts on the questions "Why Are We in Iraq? (And Liberia? And Afghanistan?)" in another *New York Times Magazine* cover story.[155] For him, this was a case of taking some distance from the instigator of war, applauding the mission, and proposing means to bring the United States back into a genuine international coalition. The war, he said, which had now become a guerrilla war, "was never simply a matter of preventing the use of weapons of mass destruction; rather, it was about consolidating American power in the Arab world."

What, he wondered, could history reveal about why America goes abroad to fight, and how could the United States "devise a coherent strategy of engagement" to meet the dangers of the new century? In a broad historical survey, he recalled that the United States had engaged in foreign wars since its foundation, "chasing pirates, punishing bandits, pulling American citizens out of harm's way, intervening in civil wars, stopping massacres, overturning regimes deemed (fairly or not) unfriendly and exporting democracy." In Latin America, in the early stages of civil war in Russia and China, in the two European wars, in Korea, and elsewhere, George Washington's pleas for isolation and neutrality had been neglected. "In fact, regime change is as old a story in American foreign policy, as is unilateralism." Franklin Roosevelt was the first US president to favour leaving the decision on threats to the peace to an international body, and even then, "a substantial body of American opinion has always questioned why the United States should ask the United Nations' permission to use force abroad." In Iraq, President Bush had acted in the belief that the constitution gave him a unilateral power of decision on going to war in his capacity as commander-in-chief. (But Ignatieff did not add that this opinion, offered to Bush by his legal advisor Alberto Gonzales, was sharply challenged by legal scholars.)

America's rules for intervention abroad, as Ignatieff saw them, were: first, "never pick on someone your own size, which in our time means someone with nuclear weapons"; second, "never fight someone who is more willing to die than you are" (the Vietnam rule, now being tested in Iraq); third, "never intervene except with overwhelming force in defense of a vital national interest" (the Powell rule); fourth, "never use force except as a last resort"; and fifth, "when force is used as a last resort, avoid American casualties" (the Clinton rule). In the nineties, the absence of any definition of the national interest brought confusion to US foreign policy, while the retreat from Somalia conveyed the impression that the United States wouldn't face a fight. "Ten years later," Ignatieff reflected, "we may still be paying the price for that mistake."

September 11, he noted, meant that President Bush had reversed rule four: force was now a first resort. "But the Bush doctrine on intervention is no clearer than Clinton's" and "burdened with contradiction." At the outset, Bush had excluded humanitarian intervention and nation-building, but he had gone into Liberia on a humanitarian mission and into Afghanistan and Iraq as a nation-builder. He had proclaimed an undefined war on terrorism, never identified the specific challengers to American interests, and "routinely conflates terrorism and the nuclear threat from rogue nations." He promised swift victories, but could not deliver them. He failed to define the rules for pre-emptive war. When was it justified?

Quoting Paul Wolfowitz, Ignatieff now admitted—as he had not done previously—that the intelligence evidence used to justify the Iraq War was "murky." "If so, the American people should have been told just that." Well, yes, Mr. Ignatieff (a reader could ask), and what did you say about it at the time? Why play the innocent bystander?

The author added that the new official line on the reason for war seemed to be that there had been no imminent danger, just a need to displace an odious regime. So "the United States is fighting wars in two countries with no clear policy of intervention, no clear end in sight and no clear understanding among Americans of what their nation has gotten itself into."

America's wars, Ignatieff argued, had always been fought for a variety of motives: economic interest, moral principle, strategic calculation, prestige, revenge. In Iraq, the invasion was partly about oil and regional hegemony, but it was also about morality. Bush is "a hotblooded moralist" who believes in freedom, and it is hardly fair for the advocates of human rights to oppose a war which "was bound to improve the human rights of Iraqis" because it is led by a man who joined the cause late.

Nevertheless, Ignatieff said, the war was not accurately explained to the American people. President Bush was "economical with the truth," which meant that the chances of convincing the public to stay for the long haul, or persuading it to agree to further interventions, have diminished.

In Ignatieff's view, America cannot afford to fight the war on terror by itself, and that means giving other nations a voice in future decisions about military intervention through changes to the United Nations. Here he fell back on current proposals for enlarging the Security Council, and on the still-pending proposal for UN recognition of a "responsibility to protect." The United States had to return to the leadership of a revived United Nations. That, he knew, was a long shot, but its failure would mean a "muddled, lurching" end to the American empire.

> Pax Americana must be multilateral, as Franklin Roosevelt realized, or it will not survive. Without clear principles for intervention, without friends, without dreams to serve, the soldiers sweating in their body armor in Iraq are defending nothing more than power. And power without legitimacy, without support, without the world's respect and attachment, cannot endure.

This essay involved a substantial retreat from Ignatieff's two-year preaching mission in praise of the American empire. The leaders of the empire had disappointed him, and its adventures abroad had proven intractable. Still, his appeals for reform sounded distinctly weather-worn, old liberal pieties in a world that would not accommodate them. He could not yet see his way out of the labyrinth America had entered; nor could he give up entirely on the empire he had embraced.[156]

On Pre-emptive War

Before the Iraq War, Ignatieff had never discussed the problem of a pre-emptive strike, though by favouring the war he had implicitly endorsed the Bush/Blair argument that an imminent threat from Iraq justified a pre-emptive attack. In

January 2004, he faced the problem in a talk to a Carnegie Council meeting in New York. He noted that a pre-emptive war is forbidden under the UN Charter (which speaks of it variously as "the use of force against the territorial integrity or political independence of any state" or any "breach of the peace, or act of aggression") and declared that the Charter's prohibition was outmoded.

> One of the problems with the Charter now is that in a world in which there must be pre-emptive military action to forestall weapons transfer to terrorists, to forestall and pre-empt attacks before they take place, either by states in collusion with terrorists or terrorist groups alone, pre-emption is simply an inevitable feature. Whatever your view of its morality, it's an inevitable part of any ongoing war on terror.

Ignatieff asked his audience to undertake "an impossible thought experiment": to consider what "any liberal democratic state would do if it had verifiable, solid intelligence of weapons of mass destruction transfer to terrorist groups, or the development of weapons that could pose a national security threat, and the opportunity arose to take those facilities out before the state or terrorist group in question became undeterrable." What would the state do? "It's clear," he said, "that any state with capability ... would act in a pre-emptive way ... The moral justifications for pre-emption proceed from our verifiable, imminent evidence of attack." (This is a version of the "ticking bomb" scenario which Ignatieff would later offer in his discussion of the ethics of torture.)

The tricky part of this recipe for pre-emptive war, of course, is his condition requiring "verifiable, imminent evidence of attack" that would be needed to precede and justify it. Ignatieff suggests that an "international consensus" on war would have to arise from "viable, well-funded, credible multilateral inspection regimes that are backed by the capacity and will to use force." The argument is circular: since this kind of unerring international inspection system is inconceivable, there won't be such irrefutable evidence, and both judgement and enforcement will inevitably fall back on the nation believing itself to be threatened or wanting others to believe it is threatened. That was the situation in Iraq, and that, presumably, will be the situation when the United States sets out on its next crusade. Does that make pre-emption morally justifiable? Ignatieff doesn't make his view clear, although he says, "we have to think in realistic terms."

The discussion obscures the distinction between what an independent critic would say, and what a member of the American administration would say, as though Ignatieff was never quite sure whom he was speaking for. (And America, after all, had already proclaimed in the National Security Strategy that it would use pre-emption on its own terms.)

Caught in an Elephant Net

In March 2004, a year after the invasion, Ignatieff was ready to offer sober second thoughts on the Iraq War in another essay for the *New York Times*.[157] Before the attack, he could now see that the American debate had been about old American wars and old ideologies, not about Iraq. "And, it turned out, nobody actually knew very much about Iraq."

Now that country was a place where Americans and Iraqis were dying, and no one could predict the outcome. Ignatieff confessed that he had supported the war "as the least bad of the available options": containment was leaky, Iraq was reconstituting its weapons ("so I thought at the time"), and they could be transferred "to undeterrable suicide bombers." This possibility was remote, but "it seemed unwise to trifle with it." If Hussein had complied with the weapons inspectors until March 2003, Ignatieff now claimed that he would have opposed the invasion. But he judged that Saddam "was playing the old games." (The UN inspectors had not said that.) France, Russia, and China weren't ready to support the United States and Britain in the Security Council; "so that left disarmament through regime change." So much, in Ignatieff's reasoning, for the UN's inconvenient processes.

The fact that Iraq proved not to have the weapons he had feared did not alter Ignatieff's view of the main issue: "I never thought the key question was what weapons he actually possessed but rather what intentions he had." Given Hussein's record, he said, there could be no doubt about those malevolent intentions. Eventually, he would certainly "match intentions with capabilities." And oil was the liquid gold that gave Hussein the wealth to buy the weapons to act on his intentions.

Bush and Blair, Ignatieff asserted, had not "misrepresented Hussein's intentions or lied about the weapons they believed he possessed." They had "exaggerated." Instead of talking about an imminent threat, they should have made an honest case for "preventive" war, to meet the long-term threat as opposed to "pre-emption" of an immediate one. But he admitted that would have lessened popular support for war even further.

Ignatieff segued neatly to his next arguments. He favoured the war because the Iraqi regime was "especially odious," and this was the only chance to remove it. The ethicist could not respect those who seemed indifferent to the price Iraqis would pay if Hussein were left in power: they were engaging in what "seemed like a moral evasion." What's more, previous American cozying-up to Hussein and bin Laden in the 1980s, mistaken as it was, "didn't make it wrong to go after Iraq." Having willed the end—to remove Hussein—Ignatieff had to will the means. Nothing else had worked.

Now he saw that the administration's intentions had been different from his: they had not bothered to plan for the occupation because they did not believe in human rights. The military should have sent in twice as many soldiers to secure order, and the occupiers should have kept the Iraqi army and police in service. Because it had abandoned the Shiites after the Gulf War, the US administration should have known American troops would not be greeted as liberators. Unfortunately, "hope got in the way of straight thinking, but so did fantasy … When fantasy drives planning, chaos results." If Washington needs so much illusion before it risks war, he reflected, then "we should be doing less intervening in future."

By now, Ignatieff was thrashing about in the elephant net he had thrown over himself. What to do in Iraq now? How to avoid American "despair and disillusion"? He appealed to his readers to remember the good news that Hussein was gone, oil was being produced, an interim constitution had emerged (this was the Bremer version, since then displaced by another one), and Iraqis were living in freedom. His final comment came close to Rumsfeld's smart quip about the chaos of Iraq: "Stuff happens." Ignatieff's version was this:

"If freedom is the only goal that redeems all the dying, there is more real freedom in Iraq than at any time in its history." No one, he thought, should be surprised that Iraqis were using that freedom to tell the occupiers to go home. Wouldn't you do the same in their place?

But would *he*? Well, no. The United States had to prevent Iraq from falling into civil war. If America falters, "it will betray everyone who has died for something better." America could not leave Iraq until it fulfilled its promise to leave the country a better place. "Now in Iraq the game is in earnest," he insisted. "There is no impunity anymore. Good people are dying, and no president, Democrat or Republican, can afford to betray that sacrifice."

Here a reader could be excused for collapsing and drawing a few deep breaths. After the intricate contortions of his half-apology for supporting the war, Ignatieff was warning all the presidential candidates of 2004 that they would have to go on supporting the war. Better, I think, that he should have written a brief letter to the editor of the *New York Times* apologizing for his error in plumping for war in 2003.

Lesser Evils

On the evening of April 28, 2004, CBS News broadcast the infamous photographs of Iraqi prisoners being tortured by American soldiers in Abu Ghraib prison outside Baghdad. The most startling of the pictures featured a hooded and shackled detainee standing precariously on a box, while others showed naked prisoners piled pyramid-style on a cement floor. In a piece of exquisitely bad timing, the *New York Times Magazine* had already printed and distributed its

May 2 issue with another cover story by Ignatieff titled "Lesser Evils." At its heart was the claim that fighting the war on terror required America to distort the rule of law. "To defeat evil," he wrote, "we may have to traffic in evils: indefinite detention of suspects, coercive interrogations, targeted assassinations, even pre-emptive war."[158]

This was not the best time for the newspaper to promote this line of argument.[159] It was already beleaguered by critics for its favourable coverage of Bush's march to war. Now it seemed to be explaining away the abuses of Abu Ghraib. Ignatieff's article summarized the dense argument of his new book *The Lesser Evil: Political Ethics in an Age of Terror* and was timed to coincide with the book's publication in the United States. Both article and book are audacious and difficult to interpret: they require close reading for a fair assessment. Ignatieff had now turned away from Iraq's worsening anguish to comment on America's dilemmas in fighting the war on terror, and as usual, he delivered mixed messages. He offered dark predictions about the potential collapse of American democracy in the face of further terrorist attacks; stern criticisms of the Bush administration for human rights abuses in Afghanistan, Guantánamo, and at home; measured support for the Patriot Act (sections of which were due for renewal or cancellation by the end of 2004); and, above all, an extended argument justifying the violation of human rights to confront the terrorist challenge.

Ignatieff opened his *Times* essay by noting the likelihood of another, more horrifying, terror attack on the United States. Repeated acts of terror at home, he predicted, would probably result in an extended state of emergency, the destruction of America's constitutional rights, and perhaps even a complete breakdown of order. That would be "what defeat in a war on terror looks like. We would survive, but we would not recognize ourselves. We would endure, but we would lose our identity as free peoples." To imagine this possibility, he insisted, was neither alarmist nor defeatist. Since 9/11, the forces of terror in the world had grown, but they could still be denied victory. To assure that, to maintain American freedom, "we need to change the way we think, to step outside the confines of our cozy conservative and liberal boxes."

Ignatieff surveyed the spectrum of rights in the conflict with terrorism. On one side, to insist rigidly on maintaining normal legal rights "simply allows terrorists too much leeway to exploit our freedoms," while on the other, to abandon rights completely in the battle would betray America's reason for being. Somewhere in the middle, he judged, a reasonable balance of liberty versus security could be found. The United States would have to "traffic in evil" to prevent greater evil, but it would have to keep the "lesser evil" it practised under constitutional control.

This commonsensical beginning was one that only an extreme libertarian would deny. The hard parts—where Ignatieff has to be questioned—are to understand the nature of the threat being confronted, to find the responses that least reduce liberty, and to assure that those temporary constraints actually function as they are intended. Using appropriate language, as well, is a significant part of the whole exercise because language can shape the public mood and define the limits of action.

Ignatieff recognized that the United States has a poor record of protecting rights in times of panic or fear, and that there had been excesses in the government's reaction after

September 11. "We were frightened, and Congress and the government weren't always thinking straight." Too many aliens had been held for too long without charges, denied due process, and deported without appeal. On the other hand, some previous safeguards of civil liberty (mostly adopted after the Vietnam War) interfered with police and intelligence activity that might have lessened the chances of terrorism. First, the timely sharing of information among agencies had been unduly restricted to prevent intelligence information from being used in criminal prosecutions. That wall, Ignatieff thought, should come down. Second, the legal ban on "targeted assassination," adopted in the 1970s, should be carefully altered. Since the early 1980s Islamic fundamentalists had been bombing American targets.

> As the enemy steadily escalated the fight, the C.I.A. needed to have operatives in the bazaars, teahouses and mosques of the Arab world, bribing, importuning and, if necessary, eliminating our enemies. Who doesn't wish we had killed Osama bin Laden in the late 1990s? But the rules on assassination were drawn to outlaw it in so-called peacetime. They were at war with us, and we convinced ourselves that we were not at war with them … [W]e may have betrayed a fatal preference for clean hands in a dark world of terror in which only dirty hands can get the job done.[160]

But those with dirty hands, he insisted, have to operate within the law: "… we need presidents, not C.I.A. operatives or their for-hire hitmen, to decide whose heads we are targeting." Ignatieff proposed a presidential directive which would set out three rules for approved assassinations: "only as a last resort, only when capture is impossible without undue risk to American lives and only where death or damage to innocent civilians can be avoided. We need to make sure that assassinations don't do more harm than good."

Ignatieff's position can be easily challenged: assassinations, or official murders, always do more harm than good. For one thing, they do so because unwritten conventions barring the assassination of leaders are a lingering reflection of codes of honour that may still, peripherally, restrain behaviour between enemies. Assassinations poison the atmosphere and encourage responses in kind in descending spirals of violence. Assassinations create martyrs. They rarely succeed in eliminating the enemy leadership, since others step forward to fill the empty spaces. By their nature, such acts of official murder must be planned and executed in secret, beyond democratic review and control by legislatures and courts. Israel's brazen policy of assassinating targeted Palestinian leaders offers abundant evidence that the policy is counterproductive. The symbolism involved in arguing that the United States should emulate behaviour flaunted by the regimes of Argentina and Chile in the 1970s and 1980s or by the United States in its own massive assassination project in Vietnam (labelled the Phoenix Program) seems bizarre.[161] Nevertheless, since 9/11, targeted assassinations have been part of the American arsenal against Al Qaeda, with unconvincing consequences. Ignatieff's endorsement provides intellectual support for President Bush's odious practice.

In the article "Lesser Evils," Ignatieff held that the theoretical balance between liberty and security could be found in the American constitutional system of checks and balances. The executive branch of government has to justify itself before Congress, and both must abide by the judgements of the courts. "Our system of government, like trial by jury, puts all coercive measures to the test of hostile, questioning review. Our system is supposed to challenge the president every step of the way." But how to do so when speed and decisiveness are vital? How can checks and balances work when terror "has to be fought in secret, and the killing, interrogating and bribing are done in the shadows. This is democracy's dark secret ... and because it is our dark secret, it can also be democracy's nemesis."

The problem, he admitted, was whether free institutions were strong enough to control a secret war, a war that the Bush White House was seeking to take even further into the shadows. (The courts had recently ruled against publication of the names of those detained in the United States after September 11, and for two years they had deferred to presidential authority in denying the constitutional rights of prisoners at Guantánamo Bay.) By the spring of 2004, Ignatieff judged, neither the US courts nor the Congress had shown the independent will necessary to control the slide towards tyranny. What good, then, in that stifling atmosphere, could pious pleading to honour the constitution really achieve?

On preventive detention, which he accepted as a necessary weapon against terror suspects, Ignatieff called for a major rule: "[T]hat no one, citizen or otherwise, should be held without access to public review of his detention by independent judicial authorities," or without legal counsel. Yet in fact the names, numbers, potential charges, and places of detention of US detainees held since 9/11 were still largely unknown. Where charges could not be made or sustained within a reasonable time, he urged, detainees should be released. (Two years beyond that recommendation, hundreds of "unlawful combatants" were still held in Guantánamo, Iraq, and probably in secret prisons elsewhere, although the names of most Guantánamo prisoners were finally published in May 2006.)

On Torture

In "Lesser Evils," Ignatieff insisted that, "The abuse we need to talk about is torture." This practice, "our founding fathers said, was the vice of tyrannies and its absolute exclusion the mark of free government." There was evidence that the United States had engaged in "rendition"—the handing over of prisoners to third countries where they could be tortured in the pursuit of intelligence, and there were further reports of torture in both Afghanistan and Iraq.[162] Ignatieff discussed two proposals that would permit the limited use of physical force against detainees: one, made by the lawyer Alan Dershowitz, called for court-approved "torture warrants"; another, defined by the Israeli Supreme Court, would allow interrogators "a justifying excuse" for torture when it had been used to extract information that had saved lives in "ticking bomb cases." But Ignatieff himself favoured "an outright ban on torture, rather than an attempt to regulate it" as the only way to maintain respect for human dignity. He conditioned this view by adding that what was needed in the United States was "a presidential order or Congressional legislation that defines exactly what constitutes acceptable degrees of coercive interrogation."

> Here we are deep into lesser-evil territory.
> Permissible duress might include forms of
> sleep deprivation that do not result in lasting
> harm to mental or physical health, together
> with disinformation and disorientation (like
> keeping prisoners in hoods) that would
> produce stress. What crosses the line into the
> impermissible would be any physical coercion
> or abuse, any involuntary use of drugs or
> serums, any withholding of necessary medi-
> cines or basic food, water and essential rest.

Such rules would be safeguarded, he suggested, by the
assurance of access to counsel and the courts for all prisoners. This statement, it appeared, was Ignatieff's basic
position on torture: forbid it, but allow for "coercive interrogations" defined by law or regulation. But what
constitutes torture? Given his formal commitment to a total
ban, the moral strength of his position rests on the kinds of
treatment he would call "coercive interrogation," but not
torture (and the circumstances in which it could be used).

His discussion of torture is briefly summarized in the *New
York Times*, but in the book *The Lesser Evil* the subject
receives an intensive, nine-page treatment. "Nobody," he
suggests, "denies that the physical torture of individuals
amounts to an ultimate violation. There is no doubt about
the moral facts ... [T]orture is the most unlimited, the most
unbridled form of power that one person can exercise
against another."[163] Ignatieff notes its complete prohibition
under the UN Convention on Torture, even during states of
exception. The book examines the moral, psychological,
political, and legal implications of torture and concludes that

it "should remain anathema to a liberal democracy and should never be regulated, countenanced, or covertly accepted in a war on terror. For torture, when committed by a state, expresses the state's ultimate view that human beings are expendable."[164] This position seems unequivocal, and it is justified. The doubts arise when Ignatieff lets something like torture in by the back door. He suggests that "it has been argued ... in so-called ticking bomb cases ... physical torture might seem to be the only way to extract information necessary to save innocent civilians from imminent attack. In these cases, majoritarian interest would seem to trump rights and dignity claims."[165]

This extreme case was the occasion for Dershowitz's suggestion for "torture warrants." Ignatieff counsels against Dershowitz's proposal, on the ground that it might begin a slide toward more common use. But he seems to approve the position of the Israeli Supreme Court (or at least does not reject it) that prohibits torture but allows a defence of necessity from an interrogator "as a plea in mitigation, not as a justification or an excuse" when the interrogator was convinced that duress was necessary to gain information to save lives. "Conscientious people," Ignatieff suggests, "may disagree as to whether torture might be admissible in cases of necessity," but "all will agree that torture can never be justified as a general practice. The problem lies in identifying the justifying exceptions and defining what forms of duress stop short of absolute degradation of an interrogation subject." He then repeats two of his previous examples of "permissible duress": limited sleep deprivation and disinformation causing stress. But he noticeably omits one practice included in the *New York Times* essay: "disorientation (like keeping prisoners in hoods)." He also adds to his prohibited list (the additions appear in my italics): "deprivation of food, water, medicine, and rest *necessary for survival, together with permanent denial of access to counsel.*" Did these changes mark a refinement in Ignatieff's views? Do they mean that he would accept *limited* withholding of food, water, medicine, and rest, and *temporary* denial of access to counsel? The reader can't be sure. And if Ignatieff himself does not accept torture in his so-called "cases of necessity," then why does he list "permissible duress" in such circumstances?

Ignatieff carried the debate further in an article titled, "If Torture Works ..." in the April 2006 issue of *Prospect* magazine. In this article, he identified "the key question" to be whether acceptable "coercive interrogation" can be distinguished from torture, and whether coercive interrogation can be divided between legal and permissible practices and others that are "inhuman and degrading." He accepts both distinctions, but recognizes the extreme difficulty of drawing the lines in practice. "I am willing to get my hands dirty," he writes, "but ... I have practical difficulty enumerating a list of coercive techniques that I would be willing to have a democratic society inflict in my name ... The issue is not ... that I care overmuch about my own moral purity but rather that I cannot see any clear way to manage coercive interrogation institutionally so that it does not degenerate into torture." He then suggests that weight must be given to the testimony of interrogators who assert that torture does sometimes work in practice "to extract information in a timely fashion." An absolute ban on torture and coercive interrogation, in such cases, "will create an interrogation regime that allows some interrogation subjects to resist divulging information and prevents our intelligence services from timely access to information that may save lives ... I do not see any trumping argument on behalf of the rights and dignity of security detainees that makes their claim prevail over the security interests (and human right to life) of the majority." The best he can do, he says, is to say that he opposes torture on the ground that this is how democracies define themselves. But after further terrorist attacks, he suggests, "a majority of fellow citizens is unlikely to concur."

No wonder readers have difficulty deciding what he means when he discusses torture.

The President's War Powers and the Spectre of Terrorism

After considering torture, Ignatieff returns, in the *New York Times* essay, to the problem of keeping the president's war powers under democratic control when pre-emptive war occurs, which it must, he says, in a war against terror when "everyone can see that instead of waiting for terrorists to hit us, it makes sense to get our retaliation in first." Iraq, he admits, showed that any decision to engage in pre-emptive war depends on speculation and doubtful intelligence, whose credibility is difficult to judge from the outside. Telling the public that leaders know best is unacceptable. In the case of Iraq, the voters were misled about what the evidence really was. "Voters must be told," he says, "what we need to know, before government commits to war in our name." For the future, Ignatieff calls for another set of rules, adopted both in American legislation and United Nations' resolutions, defining the conditions that would justify pre-emption: the danger must be imminent; all measures to avert war must have been taken and failed; and "democratic institutions" must ratify the decision. The war in Iraq, he has no doubt, failed all these tests.

Ignatieff's latest rules are feel-good and futile, and the Iraq case demonstrates their emptiness. They are abstract and vague, so generalized that they could always be redefined to suit particular cases. If leaders intend to go to war despite legislative or popular doubts or opposition (as the British chief of intelligence said in 2002), "the intelligence and facts" can be "fixed around the policy." Members of Congress are unlikely to adopt such restrictive legislation, knowing it would be unworkable, and if they were to adopt it, they would find it impossible to apply unless they were also willing to challenge the president's war powers in the courts or through impeachment proceedings. To take that ominous path, Congress would not need this kind of legislation as a tripwire. The political situation would already be desperate. Alternatively, a weak or confused Congress could be as supine next time as it was in the lead up to the Iraq War and equally ready to fit its approval to the president's demands. The administration would do all it could to prepare the atmosphere before fully revealing its intentions: it is well schooled in promoting the politics of fear. In his rules for pre-emptive war, Ignatieff simply leaves the full brew of Washington politics out of what is pre-eminently a political matter. American governments will go to war if they are determined, think they can win, and judge that they can get away with it. And President Bush's government is predisposed to do so. They practice deception as an article of faith.[166] The domestic opposition, if it wishes to halt their adventures, will have to be much bolder than it was in 2003.

Behind Ignatieff's entire discussion in "Lesser Evils" and *The Lesser Evil* lies the spectre of terrorism. The difficulty with rules of war in a conflict with terrorists, he suggests, is that terrorists (by definition) do not accept any rules. (For a start, that is a grand oversimplification that ignores much history.) Since there is no honour among terrorists, their opponents are tempted to respond in the same uncontrolled way, and terrorists hope for that kind of moral slippage. The state under terrorist siege may lose its way, and alienate its own base of support as France did in Algeria. In Iraq, Ignatieff warns, the United States could do the same unless it subjects every policy "to critical review by a free people: free debate, public discussion, Congressional review … judicial review as a last resort." Ignatieff's warning was salutary in theory, but by the summer of 2004 it had come too late. For over a year, it had been clear that Iraq was experiencing a contested occupation rather than a liberation, and an occupation that was not bringing any of the advantages promised by its idealists: not freedom, not peace, not safety, not electric power. The country had become another nightmare domain of insurgency and terror. Few in Washington were willing to recognize the situation or think about its consequences. The "critical review" that Ignatieff hoped for was totally absent from view in the Congress and Senate, occasionally glimpsed by no more than a handful of senators.

The last chapter of *The Lesser Evil* bears the stark title "Liberty and Armageddon" and exposes a fear that seems to lie behind the argument of the whole book. In it, Ignatieff wonders whether the limited, lesser evils he approves in the war on terror—preventive detention, selective killing, coercive questioning—would be sufficient or containable if the struggle grows worse. "What happens," he asks, "when terrorists acquire weapons of mass destruction? … Inexorably, terrorism, like war itself, is moving beyond the conventional to the apocalyptic."

Ignatieff worries that the modern state system, in which states have held a monopoly on violence and more or less restrained its use by deterrence, may disintegrate as nuclear and biological weapons pass into the hands of terrorists. Some of them may be "true nihilists" who lack any social base they have an interest in protecting and whose object is only to destroy. He places Al Qaeda in this category, along with "any cult with charismatic psychopaths at its head." They do not seek recognition or conventional power, but aim only to punish the United States and its allies: negotiation, concession, and appeasement will not pacify them. These are his "undeterrable terrorists." Their challenge coincides with the collapse of many states in Africa and the old Soviet empire, territories which may provide sanctuary to these undeterrables. "Evil," he warns, "has escaped the prison house of deterrence."

Ignatieff insists that this claim is no lurid piece of sensationalism and then proceeds to make it more lurid. Sooner or later, an attacker will slip through the security barriers with a terrifying chemical, radiological, bacteriological, or nuclear weapon and set it off. In this way, democracies could lose the war on terror. They need not be invaded or conquered. Rather, "a succession of mass casualty attacks, using weapons of mass destruction, would leave behind zones of devastation sealed off for years and a pall of mourning, anger and fear hanging over our public and private lives." Emergency laws would be made permanent, borders would be closed, detention camps would hold suspicious citizens and aliens. Official torture and assassination could become matters of policy, nuclear weapons could be used in retaliatory attacks abroad, and vigilante gangs could patrol the streets. This would be "the face of defeat ... We would survive, but we would no longer recognize ourselves or our institutions."

Under the pressure of renewed terror attacks, Ignatieff worries that democracy could be lost. He hopes, instead, that free institutions will be reinvigorated in time: "government by checks and balances, by open forms of adversarial justification in the courts, legislatures, and the press." But this brief offering of hope pales before his predictions of fresh terror and its disheartening results.[167]

The author sees the need for a larger program of renewal abroad to forestall his scenario of disaster: there must be increased support for democratic reform in the countries of the Arab world, increased international co-operation against terrorist groups, more effective control of nuclear weapons, and effective restrictions on any trade in materials for weapons of mass destruction. The price of these reforms will be greater costs, greater interference in free markets, and closer regulation of scientific research. All this renewal will be difficult to achieve, and will require the leadership of the United States. Ignatieff does not offer great hope for its success.[168]

So the book ends in something close to a mood of despair. But Ignatieff offers a final breath of liberal faith: "I do not doubt that we will prevail."[169]

Prevail against whom? One of the notable aspects of *The Lesser Evil* and Ignatieff's other writings after 9/11 has been his failure to probe the nature of the terrorism that confronts the United States. Ronald Steel, a professor of International Relations at the University of Southern California, had harsh words for this failure when he reviewed the book in the *New York Times*:

To describe, as Ignatieff does, terror-wielding groups like Al Qaeda and Hamas as "less political than apocalyptic" and essentially "death cults" may be comforting. But it is dangerously self deceptive. It conveniently allows us to dismiss their obvious and usually explicit political goals as simply a mask for their irrationality. It encourages us to believe that those who oppose us for our actions are "in love with death" rather than being governed by beliefs as important to them as ours are to us. By doing so it indulges us in waging "war" on the manifestations of terrorism rather than dealing with its causes.[170]

Some commentators were unrelentingly harsh in their judgements of *The Lesser Evil*. "Undaunted and unembarrassed by his broad rejection of the rule of law as we know it in the United States," wrote journalist Howard Friel and Richard Falk, a professor emeritus at Princeton University and colleague of Ignatieff's on the Kosovo Commission, "Ignatieff proposes one outrage after another, each accompanied by vague notions of legislative or judicial oversight of what amounts to an authoritarian executive power."[171] Steel added that "Michael Ignatieff tells us how to do terrible things for a righteous cause and come away feeling good about it ... He is an articulate advocate of what skeptics call liberal (or for that matter neoconservative) imperialism—the use of military power to shape the world according to American interests and values."[172] The distinguished former *New York Times* correspondent Anthony Lewis, on the other hand, wrote that "in this situation we need calm, reasoned advice on how to balance the interests of security and liberty. We have it now in a remarkable book. Michael Ignatieff brings history, philosophy, law, and democratic morality to bear on the problem. That may sound daunting, but Ignatieff is such a forceful writer that it is a fascinating book."[173] Lewis judged the work favourably by comparing the "bleak absence" of concern over civil liberties in the Bush administration with Ignatieff's sensitivity to such issues, although he did not let Ignatieff off entirely free. While he agreed with Ignatieff in his principled commitment to civil liberties and human rights, he disagreed that the jury was still out on the possible benefits of the Iraq War: "I think," Lewis said, "he is too optimistic."

Celebrating the American Mission

Ignatieff prepared for July 4, 2005, with a complex but celebratory essay in the *New York Times Magazine* provocatively titled "Who Are Americans to Think That Freedom Is Theirs to Spread?"[174] His answer is that they have done so since the beginning, when Thomas Jefferson told the citizens of Washington that, sooner or later, republican self-government on the American model would sweep the world. The promotion of self-government abroad is part of the nation's definition. Every president has proclaimed the universal value of American liberty, but Bush is the first to risk his presidency "on the premise that Jefferson might be right." He is "a gambler from Texas" who will be remembered as "a plain-speaking visionary" if democracy takes root in Iraq. Ignatieff chastises Bush for the gap between his words and his actions, for "the fetid example" of criminal practices at Abu Ghraib and elsewhere, for failures that leave "many Americans and a lot of the world wondering whether Jefferson's vision of America hasn't degenerated into an ideology of self-congratulation, whose function is no longer to inspire but to lie."

"And yet ... and yet ..." Ignatieff adds as he takes his distance from critics of the Bush administration. Jefferson's claim has shown "explosive force" both at home and abroad, and it is powerful today among Islamic democrats because "the United States actually seems, for the first time, to be betting on them and not on the autocrats." Speaking of liberty, he admits, does not make it happen, and there are many black spots in the Middle East, above all in Iraq "poised between democratic transition and anarchy." But the American mission must—and will—continue, both because it promises liberty and because it is the only surviving imperial project. Liberty often needs force-feeding from abroad, but the paradox in the United States today is that there has been a reversal of roles. Where once liberal Democrats carried the message, today the Republicans do it. Liberal Americans have become "complacent and timorous" relativists who are content to be free in America without wanting to spread their good fortune to others. Republicans have become the missionaries of liberty, and Ignatieff places himself beside them: "America is the last nation left whose citizens don't laugh out loud when their leader asks God to bless the country and further its mighty work of freedom. It is the last country with a mission, a mandate and a dream, as old as its founders. All of this may be dangerous, even delusional, but it is also unavoidable. It is impossible to think of America without these properties of self-belief."

As the coffins return from Iraq, Ignatieff knows that the fate of Jefferson's dream there remains in doubt. Yet this is where the mission must succeed "to redeem loss, to rescue sacrifice from oblivion and futility and to give it shining purpose." He has not admitted the adventure was a failure. He hopes it will not be. But he knows it may happen. In 2005, Ignatieff is no longer the brash American imperialist he was in 2001.

Nevertheless, he remains a promoter of the sole surviving world empire. "These are dangerous arguments," writes the Spanish political analyst Mariano Aguirre, "based on the one hand on the assumption that one Nation or Volk has the almost divine mission to impose a vision of the world, and on the other, that the rest of the world is either weak or corrupt, and must be redeemed by the Chosen One. An echo of the past resounds around Europe."[175] Aguirre puts Ignatieff's role in perspective:

> Michael Ignatieff has been useful to the US government as it has tried to promote democracy in the middle east. He brings to this unofficial job a special, double-edged approach: he provides conservative arguments to the liberal audience and liberal alibis to the conservatives.
>
> Ignatieff considers himself a liberal, so sometimes he criticises the Bush administration. And he is an intellectual, so he has doubts about almost everything and airs them for the liberal readers of the *New York Times*. But in the end he shares the US government's vision of the violent and compulsory promotion of democracy, the war against terrorism and the use of instruments, for example

torture, which are apparently in need of a revisionist treatment.

Admiration is at the root of this....[176]

After Kosovo, Afghanistan, and Iraq, where would Ignatieff's thoughts lead him next?

CHAPTER 4

Coming Home

Ignatieff, a "rare nexus of blueblood connections and talent," ranked seventh in a 2002 *Maclean's* feature article on the fifty most influential Canadians. The magazine described him as "a kind of citizen journalist" who had spent most of his adult life as an expatriate in the United Kingdom and the United States. "Now at Harvard," the sketch concluded, "he is circling closer to home. With an agile mind and a first-hand take on the world's trouble spots, doors open to him in the highest circles."[177]

From his base in Cambridge, Massachusetts, Ignatieff was an occasional visitor to Canada for lectures, interviews and meetings. In June 2003, as the situation in Iraq degenerated under the chaotic mismanagement of the US occupation, he was interviewed by John Geddes for *Maclean's*.[178] Ignatieff continued to defend his support for the invasion, but admitted that he had miscalculated the aftermath of war. He said that as director of the Carr Center at Harvard, he had regular contact with the US military and took their word that there were detailed plans to restore order after victory. "My assumptions were based on a lot of stuff we do at the Carr Center with U.S. military planners ... We've had conferences on this, saying, 'Have you gone through this checklist, hospitals, museums, that sort of thing?' And it was on the basis of this that I lent the war my ambivalent, heart-in-mouth support." (Reassurances offered by soldiers at academic seminars seem a doubtful basis for a decision on whether or not to support an adventure as momentous as a pre-emptive war.)[179] Now he blamed President Bush for "screwing up post-war reconstruction." Geddes wondered whether this criticism, coming from Ignatieff, was a little hasty since his January essay in the *Times Magazine* had said that "Order, let alone democracy, will take a decade to consolidate in Iraq."

There were numerous press reports in this period that the postwar planners for Iraq in the State Department had been sidelined and their work ignored under White House and Defense Department pressure. Meanwhile, the US military concentrated their attention on a rapid military victory while consciously avoiding any planning for postwar order and reconstruction. Defense Secretary Rumsfeld expected up to four-fifths of US troops to be out of Iraq by the end of June and the government to be in the hands of a new, mostly expatriate, Iraqi leadership. The expectation quickly disappeared.

Ignatieff told Geddes that the Bush/Blair decision to invade Iraq without a UN mandate was "a long overdue wake-up call" for those who still had faith in the United Nations. As he toured Canada, "what bothered me was that the only legitimacy that mattered to most of the audiences was the legal legitimacy of the UN ... Well, the UN screwed up in Rwanda, it screwed up in Bosnia—it screws up most of the time." He had told a seminar at Harvard that "the United Nations is a messy, wasteful, log-rolling organization." But he still saw the United Nations as "the best franchiser of legitimacy in the world and a very good program deliverer." What was needed was for nations like Canada to persuade the United States that its own interests were usually best served by using the United Nations.

"Unilateral empire is a bad choice for America." For Canada, there was no option other than trying to strengthen the United Nations as a counterbalance to America. "A small power has to leverage alliance memberships."[180]

Geddes reported that Lloyd Axworthy, the former foreign affairs minister who led two successful sets of negotiations to create the International Criminal Court and the treaty banning the use of anti-personnel landmines, believed that Ignatieff had given up far too easily on the UN weapons inspectors during the run-up to the war in Iraq. Axworthy suggested that Ignatieff's humanitarian beliefs "cannot be used as a license for the U.S. to do what it likes." His "new liberal imperialism" was dangerously mistaken. [181]

Ignatieff would not accept this view and insisted that the sense of urgency in London and Washington over Iraq's desire to acquire weapons of mass destruction had been genuine. As for voicing expressions of dissent at the time, he believed that "it was too much to ask the Americans to live indefinitely with even a slight risk that Iraq's illicit arsenal might be made available to terrorists."

Nevertheless, Ignatieff did not wish to lecture Canadians; he was "taking pains to be respectful."[182] Earlier in June 2003, Geddes concluded, "he was in Ottawa, privately briefing top officials on the way he sees the world unfolding. So, as usual, insiders are listening … Even for Canadians who felt betrayed by his position on the Iraq War, the chance to keep on seeing the world through Ignatieff's eyes may prove to be an experience too vivid to give up."

Nine months later, in March 2004, Ignatieff was in Ottawa to deliver a major public lecture at the Department of Foreign Affairs.[183] This was a carefully considered affair, in which he looked for the aspects of Canadian experience which could guide the country in designing a distinctive foreign policy. Some of the paper was routine Canadian boilerplate: policy should be shaped by the values of human rights, tolerance, multiculturalism, and human security, balanced with the intelligent defence of Canadian interests beside the United States and in the broader world. Maintaining Canadian independence—especially in relations with the United States—is "our guiding national interest." That means co-operating with the United States on immigration, border security, and continental defence and paying the necessary price to do that properly. "Negatively, we must not be dependent, and we must not be subservient. Positively, we must stand on our own two feet." In economic matters under NAFTA, "we cannot allow stronger partners to manipulate agreements signed in good faith to protect their own industries while devastating ours." In multilateral institutions, Canada needed to play its appropriate role, not always in the chorus. Sometimes—on landmines, human security, the responsibility to protect, and the Montreal consensus on eliminating CFCs—Canada could sing solo.

To exercise influence in the world, Canada had to have power. That meant it needed to invest "significantly greater resources" in diplomacy, intelligence, and "a combat-capable counter-terrorist and peace-enforcement force."

Ignatieff searched for the foundations of Canadian national values in the county's history of compromise and consensus-building among regions, ethnic, religious, and language groups, in the successful creation of what he had earlier called "civic nationalism": "What then is distinctive about the Canadian political tradition is the idea that the state creates the nation, that government action is a precondition both for economic development and the creation of the political community." His theme for Canada's new work in the world flowed from this core: the practice of "peace, order and good government" should now be offered as our example abroad. (Although Ignatieff did make the obligatory nod to the historical lapses of that faith, including Canada's offences against native peoples and the excessive surrender of freedom in favour of order under emergency measures in 1914 and 1970, he neglected to mention the use of wartime powers in 1939–1955 or the limitations on freedom under the 2001 Anti-Terrorist Act.)

After a quick survey of what he called "the crisis of state order" that swept the world in the last few decades, leaving in its wake a series of burdened, failing, failed, rogue, and terrorist states, Ignatieff set out Canada's tasks in foreign policy. These involve, above all, ensuring "the eventual success of the democratic revolution in our time. If emerging democracies do not succeed, we will face rising tides of immigration as well as ... disorder, discontent, violence, terrorism, epidemic disease and environmental degradation." Canada should be assisting, encouraging, and sustaining stable states with both political and technical aid and advice. It should be applying "a tool kit of preventive intervention ... conflict resolution, political dialogue, constitutional change, together with economic assistance" in "burdened" states. In collapsed societies where massacre and ethnic cleansing have occurred, Canada has a "responsibility to protect" (i.e., to intervene with military force). That phrase, he says, has entered the global lexicon on Canadian initiative. "Where one state fails in its duties, other states must step in: to stop the killing, feed the hungry, restore order and return sovereignty to those who can fulfill their duties."

To organize this vast overseas task of crisis coordination and response, Ignatieff proposed a new federal agency which would have "a prevention capability," "an intervention capability," and "a reconstruction capability." This agency, he said, would practice "muscular multilateralism"—a kind of aid with guns. Accepting this broad international duty would directly serve Canada's interest in stability. "A global order in which states are no longer able to protect their own people and their own territory presents Canada with real and growing danger. But we have the resources—and most of all, the political memory—that gives us a unique ability to turn danger into opportunity."

Once more, as on several earlier occasions in his career, Ignatieff laid out in this lecture a vast and ambitious plan for change: an inspiring agenda in the postwar Canadian tradition, some might say, or a visionary road map, others might say. But it is too vast, too ambitious, too utopian to be quite believable. Is it possible that Canada's evolution into a tolerable community, and its recent role in the world, have come about through less grandiose, more practical, more modest works of private and public effort? Does the country need this kind of bureaucratic overexertion to improve and satisfy itself as a nation?

In December 2004, Ignatieff was in Toronto to deliver a lecture on the potential and limits of American power.[184] He began, he said, "with a kind of apology. America is *not* an empire," although he had been calling it one. The United States did not have colonies, "not even in Iraq." The United States had primacy, but it lacked legitimacy: it was under challenge from Islam, and it was defying international law. In the recent presidential campaign, the electorate had rejected John Kerry's appeal for a return to multilateralism and "to the degree that it understood that option," it had rejected a gentler foreign policy for the conservative option of continuing to use force abroad. "Nothing legitimizes power like success," Ignatieff said. "Defeating Islamic terrorism is crucial to the re-legitimization of American power. Success makes friends. Failure creates enemies." But success in the war against Islam could not be assured, and in Iraq, force had created only chaos. "I don't have a clever way out," he admitted. "My business, since I'm not running for office, is to present problems, not solutions."

What he could see in US dilemmas, however, was that as American legitimacy was lost, the cost for Canada of making independent decisions was decreasing. The obvious lesson was that if Canada would pay for its ability to deploy military forces where it wants to, it would have the freedom to do so: "Any strategy to make multilateralism robust means that middle powers have to invest so that the United States can say: 'These guys are serious. These guys have come to the party with some capabilities. We don't have to do everything. We can hand missions to the Canadians—and they will do it.' "

Is this claim a bit confusing for a layperson to interpret? You bet. For Ignatieff in late 2004, a robust display of Canadian independence seemed to amount to the ability of Canadian military forces to accept cleanup assignments from the Americans. If it was a call for an expanded Canadian role in fighting the Afghan insurgents, it begins to make some sense. Still, the sense it makes is anything but encouraging. A few months later Canada did, indeed, agree to relieve a portion of US forces in Kandahar province, transforming its role in Afghanistan from NATO peace-keeping in the capital city to peace-enforcement and reconstruction under US command in the south. (NATO was due to take charge of the mission in

August 2006.) The terms of, and justification for, this assign-
ment have never been made clear to Parliament or the public.
Is Canada's role in Afghanistan what Ignatieff might see as part
of "the re-legitimization of American power"?

"An Ideal Candidate"

Five months after he delivered this paper on American
power, one of the first public hints came that Ignatieff could
be a candidate to succeed Paul Martin as leader of the
Liberal Party and prime minister of Canada. That intrepid
watchman on the lookout for potential prime ministers,
Peter C. Newman, compared the scandals facing the Martin
government with those faced by the Pearson government in
1964–1965. Newman recalled that Pearson had limped on
in power until 1968, when an outsider named Pierre
Trudeau had succeeded him, riding into the leadership on
"the credible claim that he had no involvement in his prede-
cessor's scandal-plagued record."

> Four decades later, the political earth is
> moving again, and for the same reason. The
> time seems ripe for another outsider to
> salvage what's left of Canada's "Government
> Party." That charismatic Harvard professor
> from a historic family, Michael Ignatieff,
> would be an ideal candidate. History may be
> about to repeat itself.[185]

The not-yet-declared but now potential candidate was
on a roll. A few weeks earlier, he had made a hit as the
keynote speaker at the Liberal Party policy convention in

Ottawa.[186] He was introduced by Professor Janice Stein, who described him as "a remarkably literate and versatile writer ... an innovative thinker ... the voice of our conscience, one that speaks with intelligence, one that is always laced with common sense, and most of all ... unrelenting and unremitting honesty ...The best part of this story," she gushed, "is that Michael Ignatieff is one of us. A Canadian, deep in his bones ... Michael cares deeply about this country, its past, its heritage, and its future." In return, Ignatieff told Liberals that Janice Stein was "a constant demonstration of good sound political judgement ... a national treasure." The treacle flowed thickly that evening—in both directions.

Ignatieff addressed his audience on "Liberal Values" rather than policies. He identified the party's three fundamental values—unity, sovereignty, and social justice—with Canada. Other parties represented grievances, regional, and class interests. "Our party," on the other hand, "represents the nation, ocean to ocean. We are more than a machine for winning elections. We are the governing party of our people." Under the Liberals, the country was, and must remain, "a light unto the nations," which would continue exporting peace, order, and good government to the rest of the world. At home, it would stand by the United States as the two countries that kept North America safe from terrorism. To do both of those things, Ignatieff told the faithful that the country would have to "build up our anti-terrorist forces and the combat capability of our military."

Shortly before the convention, Prime Minister Martin had opted out of participation in the American ballistic missile defense system. Ignatieff said that would be popular in the party, but he seemed to challenge the decision: "We must not walk away from the table. We must be there, at the table, defending what only we can defend."

Beyond this single line of muted criticism, and an admission that there was poverty and inequality in the country—to be corrected by continuing Liberal rule—Ignatieff could offer only praise for the party and the country it had built.

The delegates liked what they heard, and the romance was on. Within a few months he had accepted an appointment as a visiting professor at the University of Toronto commencing in January 2006, while still playing coy about running for Parliament.

The Departure of Prince Hal

Meanwhile, Ignatieff was engaged in a running argument with his colleagues at the British scholarly quarterly *Index on Censorship*, where he served as a member of the editorial and advisory boards. The first issue of the journal for 2005 included a special section on torture, advertised on the cover as "Torture—a User's Manual" and illustrated with a picture of blindfolded and shackled prisoners.[187] The section featured an article by Conor Gearty, a professor of human rights law at the London School of Economics, in which he argued that some liberal intellectuals and human rights lawyers had given the Bush administration "the intellectual tools with which to justify his government's expansionism" and had created a climate "in which even torture could be condoned." The piece was titled "Legitimising Torture: With a Little Help from My Friends." One of those he referred to was Ignatieff.

Gearty traced the steps by which "Rumsfeldians" could permit and encourage "the holding of suspected 'terrorists' or 'unlawful combatants' … in conditions which make torture, inhuman and degrading treatment well-nigh situationally inevitable." But they could not transform democratic debate without the shock of 9/11 and without the support of "a cerebral praetorian guard" of intellectuals and lawyers who would show "why there is no conflict between torture and our liberal code of laws." Gearty described Ignatieff as "probably the most important figure to fall into this category of hand-wringing, apologetic apologists for human rights abuses." He did this, Gearty said, by "the trick" of "taking the 'human' out of 'human rights.' This is done by stressing the unprecedented nature of the threat that is currently posed by Islamic terrorism, by insisting that it is 'a kind of violence that not only kills but would destroy our human-rights culture as well if it has a chance.' In these extraordinary circumstances, 'who can blame even the human rights advocate for taking his or her eye off each individual's puny plight, for allowing just a little brutality, a beating-up perhaps, or a touch of sensory deprivation?' " When intellectuals do this, Gearty argued, "scores of Rumsfeldians pour past shouting 'me too' and (to the intellectual's plaintive cries of protest) 'what do you know about national security—go back to your class work and the *New York Review of Books*.' "

Ignatieff best represents such intellectuals because he insists that evil terrorism must be fought with evil means that are excusable because they are "lesser" ones. With this kind of justification, "necessary evils" in the hands of the less scrupulous easily become "unnecessary evils." Gearty suggested that universal human rights disappear once certain people are designated as evil and undeserving of equality with others. "The wonder," he says, "is not that we good guys abuse their human rights but that we continue … to recognize that they have any residual human rights worth noticing." Gearty did not specifically accuse Ignatieff of favouring the use of torture, but only of helping to create a mood, a moral framework.

Ignatieff replied with fury in an e-mail to the editor. His reputation had been harmed so greatly that an apology was insufficient. He resigned from both the editorial and advisory boards of the journal and asked that any secondary sale of Gearty's article should be refused. He accused Gearty of saying that he (i.e., Ignatieff) favoured torture and claimed that Gearty's essay was "factually false … If your editorial staff had spent five minutes checking Mr. Gearty's insinuations against the text of my book, they could have spared me this insult to my reputation and might have protected your editorial reputation as well."

In response, the editor expressed regret for Ignatieff's distress, repeated that Gearty had not accused him of condoning torture but only of "provid[ing] a moral framework for others to do so" and offered a chance to reply to Gearty in the next issue.

Ignatieff replied: "The moral framework claim is not an argument but an insinuation that proceeds to link me with others, as you say, 'more brutal' than myself. This is what is called guilt by association, and if you cannot see that this is how you and he are arguing, I cannot argue with you." When Ignatieff asked the editor of the special section to support his position, the editor replied that the article had not been "a vindictive attack on your moral character, nor evidence of editorial negligence, nor a factual distortion."

He hoped Ignatieff would make his reply in the journal. Ignatieff has not taken up the offer.

In an account of this contretemps, the editor of *The New Humanist*, Laurie Taylor, offered two possible explanations for Ignatieff's heated response. He could have been sensitive about his reputation in anticipation of a new political career in Canada, and he could have been wounded by the rejection he faced from former colleagues in the human rights movement. So, on the rebound, why not blame them for failing to understand him, and for their editorial sloppiness? "Time for Prince Hal," Taylor reflected, "to shrug off such early flawed associates and prepare for office in Canada."[188] Reports of the affair filtered through to Canada, where Ignatieff would still not comment in late October 2005 on the rumours about his political intentions.[189]

A Canadian Leader?

Ignatieff's supporters in the Liberal Party had been searching for months to find a suitable constituency for him in the Toronto region, but without success. When the Martin government faced defeat in the House of Commons in November 2005, they had to act fast. Days before the House was dissolved, the sitting member for Etobicoke-Lakeshore announced that she would not run again, opening the seat for Ignatieff. A nomination meeting was arranged on seventy-two hours' notice, and the new candidate was acclaimed in late November, despite protests from members of the former constituency executive and the local party association. The candidate disclaimed responsibility for the untidiness of the nomination process. "Do I like the way it happened? No. Was it legitimate? Yes," he told Julian Borger of the *Guardian*.[190]

Through the long winter campaign, Ignatieff was occasionally dogged by hecklers challenging his attitudes on the Iraq War, but most of the time he managed to fly below the national radar. In their cross-country journeys, Martin stumbled over the wreckage of the sponsorship scandals, Harper reined in his wild horses, and on January 23, 2006, the Liberal Party suffered a narrow defeat while Ignatieff became a rookie member of Parliament destined to sit on the opposition benches. Martin offered his resignation from the party leadership during his concession speech on election night, and barely two months later, as widely expected, Ignatieff announced his candidacy for the Liberal leadership.

The Party's Choice

Ignatieff is a formidable candidate for the leadership of the Liberal Party. He is handsome, photogenic, bilingual, and speaks powerfully. He has wide experience abroad, an extensive network within the party, high intelligence, and no domestic record to drag him down. Those are substantial credits in the contest for the Liberal leadership.

On the other hand, his absence from Canada for most of the last thirty years must raise questions about his knowledge of the country, but the facts are subtle and difficult to judge. The leadership contest itself is an intensive seminar on Canada, and Ignatieff is a quick learner. Political understanding and knowledge, however, are not the results of a quick study; they are the products of accumulated experience. In Ignatieff's case, his political knowledge has been acquired during thirty years in Britain and the United States. At the age of fifty-nine, his political instincts and perspectives are fully formed. Both his time and capacity to learn are limited. Canadians who attempt to assess his practical wisdom and political skill lack much first-hand evidence on which to base their judgements of his approach to politics. On home ground, he has publicly considered the merits of American missile defence, but not the system of international disarmament his father worked for.[191] He has voted for the Harper government's extended military mission, under American sponsorship, to pacify southern Afghanistan. (But we do not know how he reached that position, or who would benefit from the mission, at what cost, and with what chance of success.)

What Canadians do have as a basis for judgement of the man is the ample record of his writing on international affairs. That record tells us how his views and opinions have evolved over the last fifteen years and shows us something about the way his mind works and the way he conducts an argument. In the absence of a domestic political record, these hints can be useful guides in assessing his potential as a party leader and possible prime minister.

His writings about British and American policy are confused and accommodating: he writes as a courtier in the antechambers of power, periodically adjusting his pronouncements to keep within hailing distance of Blair's Downing Street and Bush's White House. He accepted the language of an ill-defined and everlasting "war on terror" that justifies the use of emergency powers. He supported the illegal, destructive, and unnecessary invasion of Iraq. He offered elaborate but obscure musings on the use of torture. He backed American "democracy" imposed on enemies while oppression ruled among American allies in the Middle East. This was the realism of empire lite.

Ignatieff's "liberal internationalism" has moved a long way from that of his father's generation. His search for international stability led him, after 1989, from a belief that the United Nations and its agencies could peacefully assist in the creation of new democracies in central Europe and the Middle East to a belief in western military intervention to force-feed democratic nation-building. It led him from faith in the United States as the imperial agent destined to bring democracy to the world to support for pre-emptive American wars (both current and future) meant to protect the United States and its allies from fundamentalist Islamic terror. While he urges reforms in the United Nations and an American return to multilateralism through the United Nations, he is realistic enough not to expect those changes. Instead, he places overriding hope in the goodwill and power of an imperial United States, acting to serve its own interests in the world and aggressively promoting its own brand of "liberal" politics: free markets, electoral democracy, enforced liberation, all more or less on the American model. Latterly, after three years in which he justified and promoted America's role as "imperial," he has decided that the United States is not, after all, an empire: only a primary or hegemonic power.

Since the United States and its allies are threatened by the mysterious virus of terrorism, Ignatieff concedes that they must limit freedom and fight dirty in order to overcome it. To do so, he argues that the United States can legitimately engage in preventive detention, selective assassination, coercive interrogation, and pre-emptive war, because the American constitution "is not a suicide pact." Timothy Brennan of the University of Minnesota argues in response: "Everything self-contradictory in his position is rolled up in this single condensed declaration. For the constitution is precisely a suicide pact—this is what makes it a constitution. In the United States, at any rate, it explicitly confers the right on its citizens to overthrow the government, by force of arms if necessary, when the state violates the constitutional charter. If the supreme law is not a foundational pact higher than government, it is tyranny. George W. Bush, in other words, has not suspended the constitution; he has violated it."[192]

Pre-emptive war and the use of emergency measures violate the UN Charter and the essentials of democratic freedom, but Ignatieff accepts these deviations as "lesser evils" made necessary by the terrorist emergency. He has said little in his writings that seeks to understand the nature and sources of Islamic terrorism, or to place it historically and psychologically in its diverse backgrounds. Instead, he has described it as a kind of common, blind, nihilistic fanaticism that is undeterrable, to be confronted only by war. This reaction seems to be dictated more by fear and anxiety than by intelligence. It is a barrier to thought when we most need it.

In his recent writings and speeches, Ignatieff has placed Canada squarely within the world-wide system of US power as a handmaid to the American military. He suggests Canada should relieve the Americans from some of their robust efforts on the battlefield to the extent that our contingents have the firepower to do so or come in afterwards (along with the Europeans) to clean up the mess left behind. Describing this subsidiary role in the American imperial enterprise as the promotion overseas of "peace, order and good government" is misleading. Ignatieff's uncle George Grant—the author of *Lament for a Nation*, that profound reflection on Canada in thrall to liberal America published over forty years ago—would probably view his nephew's attitudes with dismay. Grant saw Canada's inability to survive in independence beside the United States as a tragedy; Ignatieff has embraced the American monolith as a benefactor while Bush demolishes the rule of law at home and abroad. Ignatieff shows no comprehension that Canada's history and character could possibly lead us in different directions from the United States or even that there *can* be any directions to take in the modern world apart from those America has divined.

His intellectual position within the cocoon of American power is reflected in his language. As a prominent advocate of the Bush administration's foreign policy after 9/11, Ignatieff repeatedly spoke to American audiences as if he *were* an American, identifying with them by the use of the words "we," "us," and "our" (e.g., "our Constitution" and "our leaders"). Since returning to Canada he has expressed regret at using these words so frequently in the United States.[193] Partly the habit may be excusable as an ingenuous effort to signal that he was a full participant in the domestic debate. But the quirk was so consistent and so emphatic that it is reasonable to see it as more than that. Jeffrey Simpson of the *Globe and Mail* speculated that Ignatieff identified himself with Americans "perhaps because few people in the U.S. care what any Canadian has to say about their problems, or perhaps because his sense of being Canadian was, shall we say, subliminal."[194]

Ignatieff's writings about nationalism, military intervention, pre-emptive war, the American mission, and the use of emergency powers contain complex, sometimes self-contradictory arguments. He absorbs the views of critics or opponents into his analyses as an indication, perhaps, of his liberal breadth, but not in order to accommodate himself to their arguments. Instead, he overrides them by assertion and holds to his original positions. He concludes his essays with ambitious calls for vast international projects which are either empty rhetorical gestures or misleading utopian appeals, distracting us from the details of daily management and modest improvement where decent moral influence can be measured. Or he concludes on notes of discouragement and near-despair, taking for granted that much of the world will stagger unaided through the coming decades in violence and disorder while the United States protects itself. These swings from hopeful vision to gloom suggest a continuing and perplexing naïveté in his view of the world.

The barbarians are at the gates of Ignatieff's world. Within Canada, he promises us a seamless national unity of equality and goodwill that undervalues our historical, national, and regional distinctions. The promise so far is vague and has as little to do with the complex realities of our national existence as his image of worldwide American democracy has to do with the real world abroad. His abstract visions, if put to the test, will feed us an indigestible mixture of pablum and ashes.

Ignatieff will be a troubled party leader if the Liberals remain in opposition through another election and become more isolated from Quebec. As a loner and without the enticements and punishments available to a prime minister, he will have difficulty withstanding attack from opponents in his own party, let alone from across the aisle.

Meanwhile, for Harper, Ignatieff is the perfect opponent. His inexperience in Canadian politics will be exposed on the parliamentary battlefield. His thin skin will be irritated by a mischievous press gallery. And in foreign policy (his special claim to fame), he will find it hard to oppose Harper's embrace of American militarism. If Ignatieff lasts long enough to inherit power, he will prove himself Harper's perfect successor. Ignatieff's imperial vision and his ambivalence on Canadian sovereignty will perpetuate the legacy of Harper as Washington's viceroy in Ottawa.

For the sake of the party, for the sake of the country, the Liberal convention should not choose Michael Ignatieff as leader in December 2006.

part two: tough guy

CHAPTER 5

The Novice

When the concluding words of the last chapter were written in the summer of 2006, the leadership campaign still had five months to go. By all estimates Ignatieff was the candidate to beat. The public opinion polls showed him as the most popular of those seeking the party's prize; and in early October, when delegate selection for the convention had concluded, Ignatieff led the charts among the nine remaining candidates for the leadership with 30 per cent of first ballot commitments.[1] The two front-runners, Ignatieff and Bob Rae, were also the most controversial candidates: Rae for his record as a former NDP premier of Ontario who was new to the Liberal Party, Ignatieff for his reputation as a liberal hawk who had promoted George Bush's war in Iraq—and as a carpetbagger new to Canadian politics. But Ignatieff's campaign consumed the most newsprint in the long run-up to the convention. The new man in town was endlessly fascinating to reporters, and Ignatieff—both knowingly and unknowingly—offered them frequent occasions for comment.

Why was he so much the centre of attention? As the unknown celebrity, now returned from almost thirty years abroad, Ignatieff was a curiosity. The other candidates (aside from the outsider Martha Hall Findlay) all had familiar political records in Canada. The national press took them for granted. But Ignatieff was mysterious and exotic. His biography was the stuff of adventure only dreamed of by the newsroom drudges of Ottawa and Toronto. They were drawn to him out of admiration and envy and a strand of intellectual scepticism. He had a talent for the bold phrase and the imperious gesture. Could this man really be the reincarnation of Pierre Trudeau that his advocates hinted he was? Established as the front-runner by his own adept publicity, Ignatieff gained exaggerated media focus and never lost it.

By early summer, the leadership campaign was proceeding at three levels. The national press generated and regenerated its own headline stories in which Ignatieff held centre stage, with Rae and Stéphane Dion slightly in the shadows, and the others mostly in the wings. At the next level, the candidates travelled the country seeking support within the party from donors, delegates, and potential delegates to the forthcoming leadership convention. And in the constituencies, thousands of volunteers canvassed for their chosen contestants.

At the first of five public forums for the candidates, Ignatieff took criticism for his support of the Harper government's motion to extend Canada's military commitment in Afghanistan until January 2009. Ignatieff told the Liberal audience that he had chosen to "stand with the troops and stand with their extension ... because Canada is a serious country. If you ask us to do something hard and difficult, we will do the job and stay there until we get the job done and return with honour.... I'm standing by a Liberal commitment." Afterwards Joe Volpe called

Ignatieff's position "made in Washington" and "Republican," while Rae reflected that "people don't want to see Harper Lite. I think that's one of the issues that is obviously going to be front and centre."[2] This reminder of Ignatieff's pro-American stance on the Iraq invasion would dog the candidate throughout the leadership campaign.

When Israel attacked Hezbollah in southern Lebanon in July 2006, Ignatieff stumbled carelessly into a new embarrassment. While the prime minister unambiguously endorsed Israel's military incursion, Rae, Dion, and other Liberal candidates called for an immediate ceasefire. Ignatieff—who was out of the country—remained silent. Finally, over two weeks into the war, in a *Globe and Mail* essay, he warned that Israel should not allow itself to be drawn too deeply into a battle it could not win. He called for Canada "to do its part in stopping this march to the abyss." Following an immediate ceasefire, Canada should propose a major international peacekeeping force to be deployed "at all Lebanese ports and land borders," along with a naval force in Lebanese waters that would "bar the entry of advanced weaponry that risks widening the local conflict into a regional conflagration." After the arrival of peacekeepers, Ignatieff called on Canada to lead a "friends of Lebanon" club to assist in "reconstruct[ing] the country's shattered infrastructure." "We are a country of peace-keepers," he concluded, "especially because we are also a country of immigrants, many of whom have come to Canada to escape the horrors of conflict. As a nation of immigrants from the zones of war, we have a special vocation for peace, and it is by exercising this vocation that we maintain our unity as a people. We have a voice that other countries listen to. Let us use it."[3] (Canada's "special vocation for peace," born of "a nation of immigrants from the zones of war," was a new and empty historical confection.)

This belated proposal annoyed Ignatieff's competitors. Rae commented tartly that: "It's interesting that Michael has waited until this point to make his position clear. The debate has been going on in Canada for the past two-and-a-half-weeks ... I hadn't heard from him at all until [yesterday]." Dion noted that the statement was late "but, anyway, coming in—is positive ... He's following me." Scott Brison accused Ignatieff of "dillydallying," while real leaders give "real responses in real time."[4]

Ignatieff responded to these complaints in a round of press interviews. His statement, he said, had been carefully timed for maximum effect. "I've been following it minutely from the beginning and watching it unfold and figuring out when was the time when a statement would be important and relevant." Hezbollah would only agree to talk when it had endured "severe military duress" from Israel. "I'm a realist," he said. "A ceasefire on the Israeli side becomes logical for Israel when it has achieved its military objectives and when it reaches the point of diminishing returns, and that is the point we've reached now." Linda Diebel of the *Toronto Star* asked Ignatieff if that turning point—either his or the war's—had come on the day that Israeli bombs killed several dozen children in the village of Qana.

> "It wasn't Qana," replied Ignatieff, formerly head of The Carr Center for Human Rights Policy at Harvard University. "Qana was, frankly, inevitable, in a situation in which you have rocket-launchers within 100 yards of a civilian population. This is the nature of the

war that's going on.

"This is the kind of dirty war you're in when you have to do this and I'm not losing sleep about that."[5]

Liberal leadership blogs—a new feature of the political landscape—exploded. "Calgary Grit" wrote: "If Harper had said that, [Bill] Graham would be purple-faced with rage at the PM's inhumanity. Maude Barlow would be self-immolating on the steps of 24 Sussex Drive. Lebanese-Canadians would be marching on every Tory riding office in the country." Liberals close to the contest began to ask about the quality of advice Ignatieff was receiving.[6] In a major speech on foreign policy the following week, Rae pointedly commented that "We cannot be indifferent or callous about these losses. We should not be calling them inevitable. On the contrary. They are a call to get out of the terrible trap into which the region has fallen. Canada needs to find its voice again."[7] By that time, Ignatieff had confessed publicly to his error. He was, he said, "ineptly trying to say simply that you can't develop policy on a reactive basis.... There've been tragedies, let's also be clear, on the other side. And leadership does not mean reacting to tragedies."[8]

Ignatieff hardly had time to recover his initiative with a thoughtful discussion paper on the reduction of Canada's greenhouse gas emissions when he was confronted with Michael Valpy's massive essay "Being Michael Ignatieff," which filled seven pages of the Saturday *Focus* section of the *Globe and Mail* at the end of August.[9] While Ignatieff's rivals had domestic political records and thus had faced "the invasive scrutiny of opposition researchers and an adversarial media," Valpy noted that Ignatieff was "the celebrity

Canadians know only from a distance."

> But who is Michael Ignatieff really? Is he the
> pinkish liberal who champions human rights
> and carries Pierre Trudeau's torch for social
> justice? Or is he the conservative realist who
> embraced George W. Bush's attack on Iraq
> and flirted with the notion that torture could
> be acceptable? Is he a family man, a man of
> faith, a man of loyalties?

Valpy set out to probe the celebrity's personality and
private life, and found a brilliant man of puzzling contradic-
tions who had discarded careers, causes, and friendships
along the way. Michael's younger brother Andrew told the
reporter of his relations with a man who had once ignored
and humiliated him:

> "I have reworked our relationship again and
> again," he said, "and now that I know him
> better, I think I can understand how he can
> have this wonderful, vulnerable, childlike
> heart, which is protected by such a ruthless,
> cold, hard, ambitious exterior. He is so much
> like my father in this way. Neither of them
> had any idea of the impact they had on other
> people.
> "Michael floats above daily interaction and
> he thinks that force of will and force of intel-
> lect can override psychological and emotional
> factors. He's had to learn they can't. The thing
> that saves my relationship with him is that we

can meet on an emotional level. His intellectual life is not real to me."

Valpy concluded his study still wondering: Would
Ignatieff be "a Liberal leader for the 21st century?" Valpy
had glanced around the new MP's parliamentary office and
noticed that, "despite a few personal touches—he brought in
his own desk and a wall of books—there's a kind of detached
look to it. Like it's a way station on the road to somewhere
else."

Ignatieff's footwork was proving awkward in the glare of
the permanent spotlight. In a wide-ranging interview with
the *Toronto Star* editorial board a few days later, he stumbled
and fell. When one editor asked: "If you lose the Liberal
leadership race, will you run for the party in the next election?" he replied: "Depends who's leader." The questioner
persisted.

> **Editor:** Have you indicated there are some
> that you would not run for?
> **Ignatieff:** No. It really is that I have to look
> at what I am looking at.
> **Editor:** Your track record, your history is
> that you move on to other projects again
> and again and again.
> **Ignatieff:** In a rival publication.
> **Editor:** Yes it's been suggested that this is
> just another fling...
> **Ignatieff:** It's a hell of a fling if it is. I mean,
> the fling stuff won't fly. It has been brutal.
> Etobicoke-Lakeshore is very very tough.
> **Editor:** But you won't commit to running

in Etobicoke-Lakeshore again?

Ignatieff: I like to serve my constituents well. But you're asking me an anticipatory, hypothetical about the situation that prevails on the 3rd or 4th of December. I am quite confident I will win.

Editor: But do you have a commitment to the Liberal party long term?

Ignatieff: I've had a commitment to the Liberal party since I was 17. And my commitment to the Liberal party continues. But there are all kinds of ways you can stay committed and involved and active in the Liberal Party of Canada without being an MP.

Editor: Without being an MP?

Ignatieff: Being an MP, without being an MP. I have been a Liberal all my life. When I go into rooms, people are glad I am in the room because people have read stuff I have written which has contributed to their sensibilities to be Liberal and what Liberal philosophy is. There are all kinds of ways I can serve the party. Don't doubt my devotion to the Liberal Party of Canada. You wouldn't do this occasionally difficult job if you weren't seriously committed to it.[10]

The interview offered an inviting target, and fellow candidate Scott Brison took aim. "These gaffes are damaging to a leadership campaign but they will be terminal to a national general election campaign," Brison told the Canadian Press. Ignatieff responded with a clarification.

"Let's be clear. I am planning to run in the next election in Etobicoke-Lakeshore. I love being an MP and I've enjoyed it enormously and I'm looking forward to doing it again." He hadn't said that when first asked, because it was a hypothetical question. "I'm ahead in the race and I plan to win. So the hypothetical is not going to arise."[11]

For the *National Post*, all this scrutiny was too much. "To read recent coverage," said an editorial, "one would think Michael Ignatieff was drowning in a sea of his own gaffes.... In fact, Mr. Ignatieff has little to apologize for. True, there has been the odd legitimate mistake ... but for the most part, his supposed 'gaffes' have really just been the consequence of speaking honestly and refusing to follow a script—a welcome contrast to most other Canadian politicians."[12] Jeffrey Simpson of the *Globe and Mail* complained that an "avalanche of coverage" of Ignatieff by the Canadian media "creates an impression of an unstoppable campaign that wavering Liberals would be wise to join lest they be stuck with a loser." Meanwhile, the ideas of other candidates were being ignored. "Is this race about Michael Ignatieff," he asked, "or is it about the Liberal Party?"[13]

The Agenda

Ignatieff laid out his campaign program in a forty-page document, *Agenda for nation building: Liberal leadership for the 21st century*, in early September 2006. This was his personal manifesto, an assertion of his belief in a "distinctively progressive political culture" that distinguishes Canada from the United States. Canada's progressive tradition, he acknowledged, contains strands emerging from "Prairie radicalism, the CCF and NDP, the women's movement and red Toryism." But above all, it derives from "the Liberal tradition that descends from Wilfrid Laurier;" and it is relevant and contemporary. Ignatieff claimed that whole progressive record on behalf of a revived Liberal Party, offering it in defiant challenge to the regressive policies of Stephen Harper's Conservative government. The new Conservative Party, he wrote, has "parted company with the common sense of their own people"; they have grown "suspicious of the enabling capacity of government itself and hostile to the egalitarian beliefs of the progressive tradition."[14]

The document was elegantly written, coherent, and comprehensive, covering the entire range of social, economic, and constitutional policies. Three years later, when he has finally become leader of his party, it could still stand (with only a few key amendments) as an impressive election manifesto for the Liberal Party—if the party dares. John Ibbitson of the *Globe and Mail* called it "audacious."[15] In a country attuned to short-term goals and safe political language, the *Agenda* offers an unusual mixture of vision and immediacy. Ignatieff was careful to say that some of his program would take time, and not all of it was appropriate for the moment. But the *Agenda* speaks of humane aspirations and offers direction. It is a document more suited, perhaps, for debate in academic seminars than on the hustings. Ignatieff was not completely at home in his new surroundings.

The commentators found the *Agenda* puzzling and difficult to absorb. At the heart of his manifesto, Ignatieff insists that "Canada is more than an economic union, more than a set of provincial economies strung out along the 49th parallel. It is a civic experiment, an attempt to bind diverse peoples together in equality of citizenship." All provinces "should be equal, but all provinces are not the same ... Quebec in particular has a unique history ... Quebecers, moreover, have come to understand themselves as a nation, with a language, history, culture, and territory that marks them out as a separate people. Quebec is a civic nation, not an ethnic nation ... To recognize Quebec—and Aboriginal peoples—as nations within the fabric of Canada is not to make some new concession. It is simply to acknowledge a fact. Nor is it a prelude to further devolution of powers."

In the document, Ignatieff calls for a new constitution— not immediately, but eventually, when political conditions are right:

> Ratification of a new constitution will require good faith and political will on all sides. When these conditions are in place, Canadians should be prepared to ratify the facts of our life as a country composed of distinct nations in a new constitutional document. The details that must be reconciled in a constitutional settlement are complex, but the fundamental principles to be respected are clear: a constitutional division of powers among Aboriginal, territorial, provincial and federal orders of government, with clear procedures for sharing jurisdictions that overlap; the acknowledgement of the national status of Quebec and the indigenous nations of Canada; the definition of a clear mandate for the federal authority to promote the unity of Canadian citizenship,

the unity of the national economic space and
the protection of Canadian sovereignty; the
constitutional definition of Canada as a bilingual and multi-national state; and the
affirmation of the primacy of the Charter of
Rights and Freedoms as the ultimate expression of the unity and indivisibility of
Canadian citizenship.[16]

"Ignatieff's Folly," declared a *Globe and Mail* editorial.

No one who survived the corrosive constitutional wars of the past two decades would ever
willingly revisit that issue. Debates over the
Meech Lake accord of 1987, with its recognition of Quebec as a distinct society, and the
Charlottetown accord of 1992, were wrench-
ing and time-consuming. National unity was
strained to the snapping point. Since those
two initiatives failed, Canada has muddled
through by making practical, non-constitu-
tional adjustments to the federation.
Common sense has worked miracles.

So it is disconcerting to see Liberal leadership contender Michael Ignatieff outline the
fixings for a constitutional package that could
bring the nation to a standstill for decades ...
    What can Mr. Ignatieff be thinking?[17]

"This breathtaking project," declared the *Toronto Star*'s
editorial comment on the same subject, "has left more than
a few Liberals wondering whether the former Harvard

academic fully grasps the depth of the Canadian public's aversion to constitutional wrangling." "Ignatieff has disqualified himself," intoned Andrew Coyne in the *National Post*:

> It is the substance of what Mr. Ignatieff proposes that is wrong. That is the true lesson of the Meech Lake and Charlottetown debacles: not that one should never propose constitutional amendments of any kind, but that one should not propose half-baked solutions to non-problems that are so obsessed with soothing particularist grievances as to leave little room for Canada. Which, as it happens, is exactly what he has done.

By the end of the week, in another all-candidates' debate in Quebec City, Bob Rae had warned Ignatieff that it would be suicide for the Liberal Party to walk into that minefield.[18] Ignatieff's venture onto constitutional ground seemed headed for an early burial. But the road to the burial ground would be decidedly bumpy.

Afghanistan, Iraq, Qana ... and Quebec

As the eight-month leadership campaign entered its final weeks, Michael Ignatieff's critics—and an increasingly sceptical press—honed their attacks. Lloyd Axworthy, the former foreign affairs minister, told the *Ottawa Citizen* that the party would make a mistake if it made Ignatieff the new leader. "Afghanistan is going to be the wedge issue in the next election," Axworthy said. "Mr. Ignatieff has shown horrible, bad political judgement on that issue. And he wasn't just a supporter of the war in Iraq, he was an outspoken apologist and advocate for it. It would make it impossible for a Liberal leader to provide an alternative to the Conservative government if he was leader. I hope he stays on as an MP and learns his craft, his trade and begins to understand what Canadian liberalism is about. And then, who knows? Maybe in the future. But to become a leader now, we would simply be taking ourselves out of the game."[19]

At leadership debates in Vancouver and Toronto, Dion and Rae again joined in denouncing Ignatieff for his belligerent support of American wars in Iraq and Afghanistan. Dion dismissed Ignatieff's vote for the Harper government's "shameful motion" to extend the Canadian military mission in Afghanistan by two years, while Rae asked: "Do you stand with George Bush on the issue of Iraq, or do you not?" Ignatieff responded, without apology, that he believed in keeping Canada's promise to the civilians and government of Afghanistan. On Iraq, he offered a refinement: he had favoured the removal of Saddam Hussein from power because of his mistreatment of the Shia and Kurdish peoples, but George Bush "has made every mistake in Iraq, and then some."[20]

Ignatieff made more difficulties for himself during an interview on Radio-Canada's television show *Tout le monde en parle* in early October. Questioned about his previous comments on civilian deaths from Israeli bombing in the Lebanese village of Qana, he expressed regret for saying he wasn't losing sleep over that, and added: "I showed a lack of compassion. It was a mistake. And when you make a mistake, even off the cuff, one must admit it.... I was a professor of human rights. I am also a professor of rights in war. And what happened in Qana was a war crime. And I should have said that, that's clear."

The storms descended. A co-chair of Ignatieff's Toronto-area campaign committee, Susan Kadis, MP, resigned from his campaign; the wife of MP Irwin Cotler announced in a letter to the *National Post* that she had left the Liberal Party in protest; and Keith Martin, MP, suggested that the candidate was not speaking for the party. "Michael is an intelligent person," wrote Ms. Kadis, "and I would think that he would have a better handle on the Middle East given his years of experience in human rights and international law." A media assistant to Ignatieff told a reporter that, while he would not retract the term "war crime," his use of the phrase had been misunderstood. What he meant—she said—was that "this was a tragedy of war, that this was a deplorable act of war, that this was a terrible consequence of war." But he would never declare a finding in international law on a talk show. Even Prime Minister Harper was tempted into the fray, suggesting that Ignatieff's remarks about war crimes in Lebanon reflected the "anti-Israeli" position of most Liberal leadership candidates.[21]

The next day Ignatieff made an extensive public statement about his lifelong support for the state of Israel:

> I have lived in Israel, taught in Israel, been an advocate for Israel. Canada is a friend to Israel.... But being a friend means speaking honestly.... I do believe that, in this explosive conflict, war crimes were visited on Israeli citizens and were visited on Lebanese civilians. As I said earlier this week, whether war crimes were committed in the attack on Qana

is for international bodies to determine. That doesn't change that Qana was a terrible tragedy that serves as a stark reminder to all that there are simply no military options left in the Middle East.

Ignatieff also announced that he would join a multi-party delegation visiting Israel in the coming month to discuss means of ending the long Israeli-Palestinian conflict.[22] (The visit was later cancelled.)

John Ivison, writing in the *National Post*, offered his capsule summary of the candidate's campaign:

> The real damage is apparent to even the most casual observer of this race: Ignatieff has repeatedly shown a worrying lack of judgement in his public pronouncements. He has made matters worse with ill-considered clarifications, corrections and apologies. These inevitably look like flip-flops and, as one veteran Liberal put it, "the most dangerous thing in Canadian politics is a flip-flop."[23]

The Quebec commentator Lysiane Gagnon, on the other hand, argued that Ignatieff's comments on *Tout le monde en parle* were no thoughtless mistake: they were carefully considered and offered with "absolute self-confidence and in a categorical tone."

> Mr. Ignatieff certainly knew this would play well in Quebec, where Israel has a bad image. And, indeed, it did. In the days following the

> broadcast, the French-language press didn't
> pick up the declaration on Qana, and the
> commentators who watched the show ...
> lauded Mr. Ignatieff's performance. This inci-
> dent shows that Mr. Ignatieff can push
> opportunism to a degree rarely seen in politics.

Ignatieff's real error, she suggested, was the old-fashioned one of assuming that "Quebec was a closed little world, and that anything he would say in a French-speaking talk show would stay between him and his audience ... without raising any fuss in English Canada." That seemed consistent with "his abysmal ignorance of modern Quebec" revealed in the same interview.[24]

One month earlier, Ignatieff's admirer Peter C. Newman had analyzed the candidate's "masterful campaign" in an essay in the *National Post*. Newman insisted that great care lay behind every step in the campaign—despite what often seemed to be "the worst kind of amateurish attempt[s] to grab headlines":

> In fact, there was nothing accidental about
> any of his remarks, no matter how casual they
> might have sounded. He may have the
> manners of a prince, but he has the mind of a
> chess master. Every detail of his strategy and
> every word of his bravura declarations had
> been carefully programmed by his retinue of
> two dozen advisors—really a private think-
> tank—which secretly plotted his strategy,
> from day to day and debate to debate. No
> campaign has been so minutely planned since
> the 1968 leadership run by another party

outsider, Pierre Trudeau, who similarly
appeared to grab startling pronouncements
out of the breezes, though he was actually
programmed down to every shrug.[25]

Ignatieff's final thrust took shape in late October.
"Ignatieff's campaign," wrote Campbell Clark, "is hoping
the way out of Israel is through Quebec." The team's new
focus was on "winnability," both in the leadership race and
the next general election. Ignatieff had placed first, ahead of
Dion and Rae, in the Quebec contest for first-ballot delegate commitments at the convention; and Quebec was the
place where the Liberal Party would have to regain ground
to return to power in Ottawa. Ignatieff counted on a solid
lead among Quebec delegates to bring him to victory. His
national co-chairman Denis Coderre explained that
"Quebecers need a reason to support the Liberals. We
cannot just speak against Stephen Harper. We must have
options to offer. And the status quo is not an option."
Ignatieff's willingness to reopen constitutional discussions,
and to recognize Quebec as a nation, were offered as the
winning bait. When the Quebec wing of the federal Liberal
Party met in conference at the end of October, it endorsed
a resolution inspired by Ignatieff's supporters calling for
constitutional recognition of Quebec as a nation. The resolution would go forward to the leadership convention for
adoption as national party policy.[26]

In Quebec, commentators warned that the province
would be "affronted" if the party rejected the resolution. In
English-speaking Canada, the alarms rang loudly once
again. Jeffrey Simpson, Andrew Coyne, William Johnson,
James Travers, and Thomas Walkom (among others)

warned that the Liberal Party would threaten its own unity and the country's if it reopened constitutional debate on the definition of Quebec's place in Canada. For Jeffrey Simpson, Ignatieff's wrong-headed positions on the Iraq War and the Quebec nation raised "the very real danger that he is, in politics, what the French call an 'idiot savant,' for which the literal translation of 'wise idiot' does not accurately convey the sense of someone deeply learned, even brilliant, but not possessed of sound judgement."[27]

The *Globe and Mail's* lead editorial, "The constitutional mire Ignatieff rashly entered," spoke of his "troubling constitutional dreams." Although he had said that Quebec would need no new powers, the *Globe* warned that the "nation" theme had become Ignatieff's campaign anthem: "I speak for all those Quebecers who say 'Quebec is my nation, but Canada is my country'."

> This is not a mere quibble over legal niceties. Every word in the Constitution has meaning. The recognition of Quebec as a nation would confer the right of self-determination under international law. True, the right of self-determination does not include the right to secede unless a nation is oppressed. But what if aboriginals in northern Quebec argued that they constituted an oppressed nation? What if Quebec invoked its new constitutional status to claim powers that it does not now possess? What if the Supreme Court, in the course of weighing these claims, did detect new powers in this new status? The possibilities are deeply troubling.

Mr. Ignatieff's vision has become a huge problem for the party that he aspires to lead. He should not have gone there.[28]

The *Globe*'s anxiety was shared by Ignatieff's fellow candidates for the leadership. The campaign teams of Gerard Kennedy and Bob Rae made it known that they were engaged in talks with Ignatieff's advisors about how the issue could be defused before an explosion at the convention. Ignatieff's director of policy, Brad Davis, confirmed that "Michael is committed to working with the other candidates to dial down the rhetoric." But Ignatieff had given a hostage to fortune. In an open letter, the former leader of the Parti Québécois, Bernard Landry, praised Ignatieff's initiative and suggested that Stephen Harper should take up the idea.[29]

In an effort to escape from this morass of his own creation, Ignatieff wandered further in with an op-ed article in the *Globe and Mail*. He repeated his assertion that Quebecers—sharing "a language, history, culture and territory that marks them out as a separate people"—constitute "a civic nation, not an ethnic nation," which deserves formal recognition by one means or another.[30] That description, responded the historian Ramsay Cook, in a tone of cool contempt, defines "an ethnic nation, to which only the majority of Quebecers belong. Cree, Inuit, allophones and Anglophones have different languages, cultures and, to some extent, histories. And 'territory' has its problems." Cook warned that "There are many more alligators in this swamp where Mr. Ignatieff wants to lead us." Another correspondent wondered "whether Mr. Ignatieff could find a way to recognize many of us living in Quebec as a

Canadian nation within a Quebec nation within a Canadian nation. I can't wait for his next article."[31]

Stephen Harper needed only three weeks to seize upon Landry's mischievous suggestion that he should steal Ignatieff's thunder on the "nation" question. When Gilles Duceppe proposed an opposition-day motion in the House of Commons to recognize Quebec as a nation, the prime minister countered with an amended motion that would recognize the *people* of Quebec ("the Québécois") as a nation within a united Canada. It was adopted with overwhelming support from all parties the week before the Liberal leadership convention. This back-handed favour allowed Michael Ignatieff and the convention to escape from a divisive trap: their own resolution could now be safely sidelined as superfluous.[32] On adoption of the resolution in the House, one Conservative minister resigned from the Harper government on principle, and other ministers were left to disagree publicly on who actually constitute "the Québécois." Ignatieff claimed credit for having revived the whole debate.

Ignatieff's Convention to Lose

The drawn-out leadership campaign was a drain on the energy, financial resources, and patience of all the candidates. Ignatieff, as the continuing leader of the race to Montreal, and the target of relentless criticism from both his opponents and public observers, showed signs of strain. Linda Diebel reported that his "much-cited gaffes and clarifications" had precipitated "a full-blown crisis with staffers flailing and morale low" just weeks before the leadership convention.[33] Despite the candidate's daily efforts to woo delegates by telephone and in small meetings across the country, his first-ballot commitments remained stalled at about 30 per cent, and estimates of his capacity for growth on later ballots remained low. Bob Rae, Gerard Kennedy, and Stéphane Dion all showed greater potential for gains once first-ballot commitments had lapsed and the contest moved into deal-making and vote-trading on the convention floor.

Ignatieff engaged in an intense final round of press and television interviews in the days before the convention, but the results were not encouraging. By now he was repeating formulaic statements about his long-time commitment to the Liberal Party ("I've been a Liberal all my life. I mean, I'm not passing through. I started campaigning for this party when I was seventeen when Mike Pearson was prime minister"), about his personal qualities ("A patriot, a man who loves his country. A man who has got international experience in a world in which every problem that comes at Canada is coming from the international, from the global context. And a person who's got guts, who says what he thinks. Tries to—knows what it is to lead."), and about his long absence from the country ("Some of the best patriots have had international experience.... Something like, I read somewhere that more than a million Canadians work overseas. Are they less Canadians because they've worked overseas and been successful?").[34]

Months of persistent criticism over his support for American policy on the "war on terror," his equivocations on Israeli policy in Lebanon, and his tendentious renewal of the "nation" debate, put Ignatieff on the defensive. His responses in these final interviews had an edgy, offended, self-justifying tone. When the *Hill Times* asked for his comments on Jeffrey Simpson's claim that he was an "idiot savant," Ignatieff snapped back:

> I won't comment on what columnists have to
> say, and I can hardly believe that mine is the
> only judgement at issue in this convention.
> We've got eight candidates and their judge-
> ment should be subjected to the same scrutiny
> that mine has been subjected to. The second
> thing to say is that people have to understand
> why I'm in front. I'm in front because people
> like my judgement. They like my judgement
> on the environment. They like my judgement
> of the importance of reducing the gap
> between rural and urban Canada. They like
> my judgement that the Liberal Party of
> Canada has to reach out to Quebec Liberals,
> national unity Liberals, Liberals who want to
> maintain the community of our country and
> respect what is specific and distinct about
> them. They like the ... judgement of mine
> which has been lead from the front and lead
> with ideas.[35]

Anne Kingston, in a *Maclean's* feature article, described Ignatieff as a romantic intellectual—brooding, tormented, inclined to sentimentalize the people and causes he admires, perpetually subject to disappointment, inclined always to pass on to the next great cause.[36] On the contrary, Ignatieff told the CBC's Evan Solomon, he is no dreamer: "I am a prudent man, I'm a responsible man in politics.... I'm in politics to face facts," rather than to create unnecessary turmoil.[37] But facts are facts, and they require courageous leaders to face them.

Pollsters and reporters could not predict the outcome of the leadership race. It was impossible to enter the minds of 5,000 delegates to the Liberal convention as they consulted with each other and reflected on their final choices. The party had been riven by a long war between the Chrétien and Martin factions; now it was further dislocated by scandal and the loss of power. Who could say how these delegates, released from the disciplines of power, might behave? The money and influence seemed to be with the newcomers Ignatieff and Rae. There was talk of deals (especially between the second-tier, non-establishment candidates Gerard Kennedy and Stéphane Dion) as the convention opened. But after the first ballot, nothing was predictable. There was reasonable consensus—based on all the quietly troubling doubts about the judgement of the front-runner—that Ignatieff could not achieve majority support at the convention. He remained the unknown (though slightly battered) celebrity. Many delegates knew little about him beyond the headlines, the campaign propaganda, and the hyped enthusiasm of his boosters. In Montreal, as they gathered for four days at the end of November, the waves of uncertainty were about to take control.

Michael Ignatieff's supremely self-assured organization set out to manage the mood of the convention and sweep away doubts. The political observer Robin Sears described their efforts:

> The lessons of hubris often flay the most powerful and well-financed in politics. The Ignatieff floor organization, backed by a 30-person call centre in the bowels of the convention hall, hundreds of workers and a

delegate tracking system honed over months of intelligence gathering, was an impressive sight. The Ignatieff presence was overwhelming from day one. Ignatieff greeters at every door of the Palais des Congrès welcomed every delegate. Each bleary morning the first thing that delegates saw on stumbling out of their hotel rooms was the Ignatieff News delivered pre-dawn to thousands of rooms. Their red-scarved minions carpeted the floor of the convention, the party rooms and hotel lobbies.

Detailed briefing sessions were held twice a day for team captains, with precise instructions about how to deliver the session's spin and how to fight others' counter-spin. Leadership campaign budgeting is always an elegant confection of fiction, misdirection and ironically misnamed expenditures, so it is impossible to cost such a convention machine. Veterans of previous wars, observing the firepower, debated whether it was "high six figures or low sevens"....

A successful leadership campaign is a delicate mix of money, muscle and the blackest of political arts. Candidates issue vapid policy pronouncements and memorize a few lines about each of the most gripping policy itches of the day, but it is to the best organizers that victory most often goes. Unless they are flogging an indigestible product, as this event amply illustrated.[38]

For four days and nights the candidate was everywhere, at the congress centre, in the delegates' hotels, and in meeting rooms. Ignatieff and his wife Zsuzsanna Zsohar carried their crowds with them, sweeping down the escalators into the congress hall at the head of a tide of supporters, smiling and gesturing as the wave swept them forward.

On the morning after the candidates' speeches were delivered, Jeffrey Simpson reported that Michael Ignatieff had "set the agenda for the campaign" but had also divided the party most deeply.

> Michael Ignatieff delivered the best speech at the Liberal convention last night—eloquent, passionate, nicely crafted—that nonetheless left a majority of the crowd almost stone cold.
>
> In a telling reaction, his delivery and content galvanized his supporters, whereas everywhere else, even his best lines barely sparked any clapping.
>
> When other candidates spoke about the challenge of climate change, delegates everywhere applauded, but when Mr. Ignatieff did so, more than half the hall barely responded. The same reaction attended his other themes, all of which are popular with Liberals.
>
> The reaction reflected what has happened in the party going into today's vote. Mr. Ignatieff is the polarizing candidate, the preferred candidate of the majority of the party establishment and a figure of electrifying promise to many delegates, but also the candidate who inspires tremendous resistance from other delegations.[39]

In the end four events—and all the complexity that lay behind them—were enough to give Stéphane Dion the leadership: his achievement of third-place standing behind Ignatieff and Rae on the first ballot, just two votes ahead of Gerard Kennedy; Kennedy's quick decision, after the second ballot, to withdraw and urge his delegates to support Dion; Ignatieff's loss of his first-place lead to Dion on the third ballot; and Bob Rae's decision (when eliminated on the third ballot) not to give any direction to his delegates, who split roughly two-to-one in favour of Dion on the final ballot.

	1st ballot	2nd ballot	3rd ballot	4th ballot
Ignatieff	1412(29.3%)	1481(31.6%)	1660(34.5%)	2084(45.3%)
Rae	977(20.3%)	1132(24.1%)	1375(28.5%)	
Dion	856(17.8%)	974(20.8%)	1782(37%)	2521(54.7%)
Kennedy	854(17.7%)	884(18.8%)		
Dryden	238(4.9%)	219(4.7%)		
Brison	192(4%)			
Volpe	156(3.2%)			
Hall Findlay	130(2.7%)			

Perhaps Ignatieff and Rae knocked each other out of the ring; perhaps the lingering doubts about Ignatieff on the convention floor were enough to deny him victory. As the fourth round of balloting began, his team knew that he could not win.

Michael Ignatieff's stricken face marked his loss as he awaited final announcement of the results on the convention floor that Saturday afternoon.[40] But he'd recovered by the time he reached the stage to offer generous words of praise for Stéphane Dion. "We have chosen a man of principles," he said, "a man of courage and a man of conviction. He will have my entire support."[41]

CHAPTER 6

Deputy Leader

After the defeat, Michael Ignatieff had no intention of slipping gently into the parliamentary background. When Stéphane Dion invited him to write the party's electoral platform, he reflected briefly, then declined the offer. Ignatieff told Dion that, since the new leader already knew the policies he wished to promote, there would be no challenge in the job. Instead, Ignatieff chose his own role: he wished to be deputy leader of the party. "I want to be part of the team," he told one of Dion's aides, "and being deputy leader we can work together more." Dion acceded. When Jane Taber reported the appointment in the *Globe and Mail*, she wrote that Ignatieff had been "receptive to the offer of the position of deputy leader right away," without mentioning that the proposal was his own. Bob Rae (who was not yet an MP) took on the policy chairmanship.[42]

Once the leadership campaign ended in December 2006, all the candidates except the winner virtually disappeared from the headlines. That was especially true for Bob Rae, Gerard Kennedy, and Martha Hall Findlay, who did not have parliamentary seats. Michael Ignatieff remained more prominent as deputy leader in the House; but that was a routine role whose work took place largely behind the scenes. In public there were only infrequent occasions to assess the evolution of his ideas and his judgement. In his new role, he was writing and publishing less; when he did speak publicly, his responsibility as a formal party spokesman usually tempered his remarks.

In the House of Commons, Ignatieff followed Dion in the daily question period. Questions normally arose from the morning's newspaper headlines—and in accord with recent habit they were combative and repetitive. The new Liberal front bench did little to raise the quality of discussion in question period, while Prime Minister Harper's front bench worked intrepidly to lower it. There was much shouting and flailing of arms. The Speaker sat glumly in the middle, unable to impose decorum without the authority of the House to back him. The opposition was not in a search for facts, but for political advantage and nightly news headlines. This—as Ignatieff was later to write—was all theatre. Dion and Ignatieff invited daily comparison as, one after another, they harried Harper and his ministers: Dion, his mouth taut, his voice high, his words indistinct and often mispronounced, seemed painfully out of place; Ignatieff, his voice strong, his expression furious, his words pointed, overshadowed his front-bench partner. But both played from prepared scripts, failing to adjust their supplementary questions to the government's tendentious answers, and sometimes repeating the same questions day after day. In this vaudeville performance, Ignatieff showed a presence that Dion lacked. Through 2007 and 2008 Ignatieff grew more confident in his role; Dion never could match the histrionics of the deputy sitting at his left shoulder.

Inside the House and beyond, Harper's Conservatives did everything they could to sharpen the comparison between

Dion and Ignatieff—always to the leader's disadvantage. Dion (said the Conservative attack ads) was not a leader. On the environment and the Kyoto Accord, Conservative ads revived the image of Ignatieff rebuking Dion for the Liberal record on the environment during the leadership debates: "We didn't do it, Stéphane!" One day in February 2007, when Dion was absent from the House and Ignatieff led off question period, Prime Minister Harper could not resist an easy shot: "What is clear," he mocked, "is that the Honourable Member certainly has a plan to audition for a new role."[43]

Dion's intimates were sensitive to the opposition leader's insecurity. Three months after the convention, Dion's choice as the new national director of the party, Jamie Carroll, told Linda Diebel that Rae, Kennedy, and Ignatieff were all potential challengers for the crown. He agreed that the knives were not yet out—and yet he worried. "All three of them have legitimate claims to being the next guy.... What they do in public doesn't bother me. It's the shit they do behind the scenes—which I may not know they're doing—that keeps me up at night."[44]

For Ignatieff, the deputy leadership offered chances to build his influence in the national party unavailable to anyone else but Dion. Ignatieff travelled the country fulfilling engagements at party and public meetings, constantly plugging the historic role of the Liberal Party in building a progressive nation and decrying Conservative efforts to destroy it. He was (not so subtly) paying his dues to party and country, demonstrating his commitment to the homeland he had left thirty years before, erasing one of the marks against him in 2006. He was here to stay. And he was maintaining his extensive Liberal networks.

As it became more and more clear that the party's choice of leader was dubious, the likelihood of another leadership contest was never far from anyone's mind. No one—except, perhaps, Stéphane Dion—thought the party was about to witness a repetition of the 1990s, when Paul Martin waited through more than a decade and three general election victories before he could challenge Jean Chrétien's grasp on power. The Conservative government's popularity was not growing, but neither was it decaying. The sense of an inevitable Liberal return to office, which had survived the defeat of January 2006, was fading. But that did not spawn any active conspiracies against the new leader. Not yet. No one needed them; no one could risk them. Instead, the latent conflict for power revealed itself in uncertainty and mixed signals over when the minority government should be defeated in the House.

Despite Stéphane Dion's public insistence, the Liberal Party was unprepared for a general election in 2007. The leadership candidates all had substantial debts to be repaid, as did the party; the organization was ragged; and the new leader's policies had not yet been elaborated. The party feared an early election under Dion, but recognized he would have to be given his chance. Fairness demanded that—but barring miracles, he would have just one chance, not Chrétien's three. The political logic of this situation, while obvious, could not be openly debated. But for aspiring leaders—whatever the risks—there was bound to be some temptation to go into an early general election that would almost certainly be lost. This would clear the decks. The most likely successors, Michael Ignatieff and Bob Rae—who had both entered their sixties—had the most to gain from going early to the polls. Others had more time.[45] Through

2007, the party chose to wait.

Periodically the press gallery reported rumours of rumbling within the caucus, which were always officially denied. When Dion and the Liberal Party lost three Quebec by-elections in September 2007, the gossip among "bloggers and unnamed sources" pointed to the damaging influence of "shadowy figures supposedly loyal to [Dion's] former leadership rival, Michael Ignatieff." But Dion claimed that the enemy he faced was not within the party: it was the caricature of himself in the Conservative attack ads. "I have to fight with a Stéphane Dion who doesn't exist," he exclaimed. Yet the rumours of internal dissent persisted.[46] A few weeks later, when Dion spoke in the House in response to the Harper government's Speech from the Throne, close observers—including Sheila Copps—noticed that as Dion stumbled awkwardly through his remarks, Ignatieff smirked, rolled his eyes, guffawed, and hid his face in his hands. "With Ignatieff's poorly disguised glee," Copps wrote, "don't expect the haemorrhaging in the Liberal party to end any time soon."[47] The caucus was enduring, not enjoying, Stéphane Dion's leadership.

A Confession

In what he said was "a culmination of a long period of rethinking,"[48] Michael Ignatieff returned to the pages of the *New York Times Magazine* in August 2007 with a major essay, "Getting Iraq Wrong." "The unfolding catastrophe in Iraq," he wrote, "has condemned the political judgement of a president. But it has also condemned the judgement of many others, myself included, who as commentators supported the invasion."[49]

More than four years after the invasion of Iraq, this was a confession long delayed. Ignatieff framed it by explaining that now, as a practising politician, he had to improve on the judgements he once offered as an academic. Academics, he wrote, can afford to have fun playing with interesting ideas, taking them "wherever they may lead." But politicians have to be practical. "Politicians cannot afford to cocoon themselves in the inner world of their own imaginings. They must not confuse the world as it is with the world as they wish it to be. They must see Iraq—or anywhere else—as it is." This was disingenuous. Ignatieff neglected to say that his original commitment to war in Iraq was made, fervently, not in an academic classroom but in the same pages of the *New York Times Magazine*. It was made consciously as a political statement, as advocacy, not as an innocent academic exercise.

Barely into his confession of bad judgement, Ignatieff took off into the stratosphere, glorifying the intuitions of great politicians. For after all, they are not simply realists:

> Like great artists, great politicians see possibilities others cannot and then seek to turn them into realities. To bring the new into being, a politician needs a sense of timing, of when to leap and when to remain still. Bismarck famously remarked that political judgement was the ability to hear, before anyone else, the distant hootbeats of the horse of history. Few of us hear the horses coming.

Then it was back to the Iraq of 2007, where America's

hard choice was to stay or to leave. If the Americans stayed, Ignatieff insisted, they would bear the cost; if they left, Iraqis would (mostly) bear it. That suggested "how American leaders are likely to decide the question." Ignatieff seems to mean that, on the issue of "cost," the US would decide to leave Iraq—although he does not quite say it. (This whole oversimplified analysis is palpably false. In 2007, as he wrote, the Bush administration was struggling to avoid accepting any timetable for departure—and all the proposed timetables under discussion were deceptive in that they included plans to keep large American bases and contingents permanently in Iraq, though not in battle. Twenty months later, in 2009, under a new president, the American presence in Iraq remains massive, the possibility of full withdrawal unlikely, and the human and material costs immeasurably high on both sides.) In any case, Ignatieff admitted, the choice in Iraq had to be based on the recognition "that all courses of action thus far have failed." Where that insight might lead, he failed to say.

Quoting Samuel Beckett and Niccolò Machiavelli on "the inner obstinacy necessary to the political art," Ignatieff argued that political judgement must ruthlessly overstep the limits of ordinary ethical action. Politicians must be tough and sometimes mean. They must know how and when to do wrong, but they must still be judged by the ordinary rules.

The academic/politician then turned to what seemed to be a reflection on harsh personal experience of the brutal life faced by politicians. (A reminder to his former academic colleagues—and all the rest of us—about the awful risks he had taken in making the journey into politics?) Politics is cruel. Politics is theatre; as a politician one must "pretend to have emotions that you do not actually feel." And in that theatre of false emotion, there is no room for kindness.

> In public life, language is a weapon of war and
> is deployed in conditions of radical distrust.
> All that matters is what you said, not what you
> meant. The political realm is a world of
> lunatic literalism. The slightest crack in your
> armour—between what you meant and what
> you said—can be pried open and the knife
> driven home.

Next came a warning to his constituents, with a bow to
Edmund Burke: he would sometimes sacrifice his judgement
to theirs, but he would never sacrifice his principles. (The
New York Times Magazine seems a curious place for this
message to the electors of Etobicoke-Lakeshore.) But principles, of course—if they are dogmatic—are "usually the
enemies of good judgement. It is an obstacle to clear thinking to believe that America's foreign policy serves God's plan
to expand human freedom.... Politicians with good judgement bend the policy to fit the human timber." (A crack at
George Bush and a bow to Immanuel Kant all in one!)

So, Ignatieff tells us, let us be prepared for the messy
compromises of politics. The good politician himself will
not be happy with the compromises he makes; but good
compromises restore peace, while bad ones surrender to
compulsion or force. (This abstract statement, without
specific references, is nothing more than empty tautology.)

Quickly now, back to the issue of Iraq and "who best
anticipated how events turned out." It turns out that "many
of those who correctly anticipated catastrophe"—that is,
most critics of the invasion—were not exercising their good

judgement, they were "indulging in ideology. They opposed the invasion because they believed the president was only after the oil or because they believed America is always and in every situation wrong." (Take that, you who dared to oppose the war!)

Those who "truly showed good judgement on Iraq" correctly predicted the result, *and* correctly judged "the motives that led to the action. They did not necessarily possess more knowledge than the rest of us." (Ignatieff takes for granted that "the rest of us" failed this test.) "They" (those few remaining and unnamed, who were of truly good judgement in opposing the war) were unlike President Bush, who took wishes for reality, who assumed that since his motives were good everyone in the Middle East would believe him good as well. "They" didn't assume that a free state could rise out of years of police terror, or that America could shape reality in a distant land it knew little about, or that it had to defend rights and freedom in Iraq because it had done so in Bosnia and Kosovo. "They avoided all these mistakes." (It's a long list just to show how difficult it is to qualify as one of "them.")

Ignatieff finally confesses that "I made some of these mistakes and then a few of my own." The lesson he has drawn is to be "less influenced by the passions of people I admire," such as Iraqi exiles, or Kurds. "Good judgement in politics, it turns out, depends on being a critical judge of yourself," on being able to override your own emotions. The president lacked that quality, for he "had led a charmed life, and in charmed lives warning bells do not sound." Ignatieff, the charmed academic, lacked it too.

But now, we know—because he has told us—he is a politician, and presumably a wise one who has learned his lesson.

He knows politicians must "listen to the warning bells within." He must be a tough guy who rises above emotion. He will henceforth be prudent. But prudence cannot inspire a people.

> Democratic peoples should always be looking for something more than prudence in a leader: daring, vision and—what goes with both—a willingness to risk failure. Daring leaders can be trusted as long as they give some inkling of knowing what it is to fail. They must be men of sorrow acquainted with grief, as the prophet Isaiah says, men and women who have not led charmed lives, who understand us as we really are, who have never given up hope and who know they are in politics to make their country better. These are the leaders whose judgement, even if sometimes wrong, will still prove worthy of trust.

If the suit fits, as they say, wear it.

Ignatieff's essay has the intricate musical flow of a rondo on the theme that he has discarded foolish academic things and found wisdom as a politician. He has discovered his vocation—tough as it might prove to be. On balance, his admission of error over Iraq turns out to be a minor point in the essay; what we are meant to know is that he is a changed man. As music, this melody would be an elegant diversion; as serious argument, it is pretentious and intellectually ramshackle. As a first example of Michael Ignatieff's pledge to depend less on personal emotion and more on practical realism in his contributions to public debate, it was not a promising beginning.

The article was widely commented upon. An editorial in the *Toronto Star* noted that Ignatieff put on "a credible sack-cloth-and-ashes show for his American readers, mincing no words about just how badly he goofed.... The Iraq mess has taught him to value prudence in leadership, as well as vision and daring. 'I blew it, but I've grown,' he seems to say. That, surely, is not a message that Americans would be especially interested in hearing. Rather, it seems aimed at a Canadian audience, looking for leadership they can trust."[50] Joey Slinger, the *Star*'s resident humorist, reflected that Ignatieff had taken his readers along "on one of his Boy Scout rambles through his inner self," but had missed the main point: he was not just a supporter of the Iraq War but "one of the foremost enablers."[51] Robert Sibley, writing in the *Ottawa Citizen*, argued that Ignatieff's essay "demonstrates the opposite of what he claims to have acquired since entering the political arena—political judgement," since Ignatieff "never actually says in any detail why he thinks the Iraq invasion was a mistake, beyond accusing President George W. Bush of not knowing what he was doing."[52] The *Montreal Gazette*, on the other hand, commented that the article was "a refreshing and thought-provoking glimpse at how an intelligent person copes with the challenges of policy decision-making," while the paper's political columnist Don Macpherson suggested that Ignatieff's "meandering rumination" was really intended as his claim to take the Liberal Party from the shaky leadership of Stéphane Dion.[53] Two academics at McMaster University argued that most academics got the argument over the Iraq War right, and that Ignatieff's claimed distinction between academic and political judgement was false. His mistake, they said, "was not that he was isolated from the real world, but that he betrayed the liberal principle that the ends cannot justify the means.... [I]t was likely that Mr. Ignatieff's political instincts and ambitions, not his academic training, moved him then, as now, to support the conventional wisdom of powerful elites in the US and now back home in Canada."[54] An essayist in *The Nation* described Ignatieff's article as a "long, woolly, pompous pseudo-confession," while David Rees, in a massive and hilarious putdown on the *Huffington Post* website, called it a story of the hero's long march "from the theory-throttled, dusty tower of academia to the burned-out hell-hole of representative politics. Danger lurks. Grime abounds. The narrative tension is: *Can the hero be wrong about everything, survive, and still convince people he's smarter than everyone in Moveon.org?*"[55]

Two Liberal MPs who had supported Michael Ignatieff's bid for the leadership, Denis Coderre and Paul Zed, denied the possibility that the reversal of his view on the Iraq War was meant as "an effort to reposition himself for a bid to unseat or succeed Mr. Dion." Instead, said Zed, it would help Dion to "have everybody lined up on such an important world issue." "Michael Ignatieff is a model of loyalty and dignity," added Coderre. What Ignatieff's article demonstrated was that "he wants to remain in public life, and I'm very pleased about it."[56]

"This is not an insurrection"

When the Liberal caucus held its annual summer retreat in Newfoundland at the end of August 2007, Michael Ignatieff was in a playful mood. The party's MPs, Senators, and press followers had been taken on a whale-watching excursion at a time when there were no whales to be seen. Don't worry, Ignatieff told reporters, there were lots of puffins, and "the puffin is a noble bird." As the caucus concluded the next day, members of the scrum asked him to expand on his praise for this "oddball orange-billed aquatic bird." Ignatieff took their goading in good spirit.

> It's a noble bird because it has good family values. They stay together for 30 years. I'm not kidding. They lay one egg and they put their excrement in one place. They hide their excrement. They hide their excrement! They have good family values. They flap their wings very hard and they work like hell. This seems to me a symbol for what our party should be.
>
> Noble in my lexicon means underappreciated as well. The puffin is not anybody's hero right off the bat, but you see his little flappy wings and how hard it works and the good family values, and you start to warm to the puffin.
>
> And that is the last thing I'm saying about puffins.

The *Toronto Star*'s Susan Delacourt lamented the fact that Ignatieff's amusing little speech had caused scandalized comment. Critics asked how a Liberal could compare his party to a bird that hides its excrement. What would the Tories make of that? Delacourt wondered where the humour had gone in Harper's Ottawa. The prime minister was "definitely not funny." And Stéphane Dion was "similarly humour challenged." While Ignatieff talked of the family values of puffins, Dion had earnestly compared the whale-less waters of Bay Bulls, Newfoundland, with the whale-filled waters of La Malbaie, Quebec where the caucus would meet in 2008. If that was wit—she exclaimed—it "seemed a little lost on the crowd."[57]

Through the autumn of 2007, the Liberal Party under Stéphane Dion's leadership continued to dodge opportunities to defeat the government in the House. At year's end, Dion told Craig Oliver of CTV news that "I personally found it very difficult to not vote down the government, but after discussing it with my team, I decided Canadians did not want an election in 2007." But perhaps the mood was changing. "After two years of this minority Conservative government," he said, "people may not want, necessarily, an election, but they will not be surprised if there is one.... If there is an election—I know you will ask me the question, and I don't know the answer more than you."[58]

When Jim Flaherty presented the 2008 budget in late February, Dion still didn't know the answer more than you. He told reporters that the Liberal Party would disagree with the budget, but "we'll find a way to not defeat the government.... We have a very unanimous view ... we'll choose our time, we'll choose our issues to go to election and to win it." The Liberal amendment to the budget motion blamed the government for "an NDP-like lack of fiscal prudence," which guaranteed that at least one of the opposition parties would vote against it, which would assure its defeat. On the main motion, the Liberals would repeat their demoralizing practice of arranging for enough abstentions to assure that the government would have its majority.

The caucus was losing its coherence. Both Dion and Ignatieff (along with many other Liberal MPs) initially favoured an early election triggered by the budget vote. But in an urgent strategy meeting, Ralph Goodale and Senators David Smith and Céline Hervieux-Payette convinced Dion that the party lacked the money, organization, and candidates to win an election. (They had also assured that the national organization would do nothing to begin preparations for a campaign, ignoring a directive from the leader.) Ignatieff argued strongly in favour of an early election, while Dion was persuaded to change his mind and avoid one. When Dion went before the cameras to explain the party's position on the budget, Ignatieff refused to join him. Dion was confronting a passive revolt on both sides of the question: an organization that would not follow him, and caucus colleagues whose loyalty was near to exhaustion because of his turnabouts. Jack Layton described Dion as "the leader of official abstention," while Stephen Harper began referring to Layton as leader of the official opposition.[59]

The most contentious issue in foreign policy facing Canada during these years was the country's role in Afghanistan. Canada's contribution to the American assault after 9/11 was initially small and symbolic, but it evolved through three stages into a substantial, primarily military operation in Kandahar province by mid-summer 2005. When the new Conservative government sought to extend the mission by two years in early 2006, Michael Ignatieff and two dozen of his colleagues bolted to support the government against the majority in the Liberal caucus, who opposed any extension—an early indication of Ignatieff's wish to be known as the tough guy among the leadership candidates.[60]

Stephen Harper had chosen the Afghan mission as one of the markers—perhaps the sole marker—of his foreign policy.

He knew it was a potentially divisive issue for the Liberal Party, who were responsible for Canada's initial engagements in that pitiless land; but failure could also threaten his own record. The military outlook deteriorated in 2006 and 2007 as the Taliban revived and extended their guerrilla campaign against the Karzai government and its foreign supporters. Canadian troops in Kandahar faced continuing and deadly attack. At home, opinion about the mission remained divided as the prospects for success faded. Getting out or staying in posed equally perplexing political risks.

In the fall of 2007, Harper made an adroit political move by naming the retired Liberal minister John Manley to chair an independent study group on Canada's role in the country. Pending the panel's report in January 2008, the issue would be off the table; and at best the report might propose some longer-term means of defusing this political time bomb. The panel reported in January 2008, recommending a "conditional extension" of the Canadian mission beyond February 2009, dependent on commitments of further troops in Kandahar province from other NATO countries, the provision of airlift helicopters and drones to assist Canadian forces, an expansion of non-military assistance, and improved official reporting of Canada's efforts.[61]

Manley had given Harper the arguments he needed both at home and abroad; and the prime minister quickly proposed a motion to extend the mission to the end of 2011, subject to Manley's conditions. This was a direct challenge to Stéphane Dion's call for withdrawal of Canada's forces by the existing deadline of February 2009. The motion could not be easily opposed by Liberal MPs, since it was based upon proposals from a respected Liberal ex-minister. It caused predictable turbulence in the Liberal caucus. Did

Manley command more loyalty than Dion? Ignatieff took the lead in drafting a long Liberal amendment, which prompted the government to revise its motion to incorporate most of the Liberal draft. On March 13, 2008 the House endorsed the motion by an overwhelming vote of 198 to 77. The Bloc and NDP opposed; most Liberals supported the government; but twenty Liberals did not show up for the vote. Afghanistan was thus erased from the Canadian political agenda, while conditions on the battlefield grew worse. Effectively, the Canadian military role in the war was extended by three years. Dion (who, in 2006, had opposed extension beyond 2007) suffered severe political embarrassment, while Ignatieff shared credit for a piece of neat political management with Harper and Manley. The affair left Dion's authority in the party still more tenuous.[62]

Dion's hold on the party disintegrated further in March, when he claimed at a meeting with his Quebec executive that support was growing in the province at the very moment that the latest CROP poll showed the Liberals running a weak third behind the Bloc and the Conservatives. Accusations flew. A Dion supporter at the meeting accused Ignatieff of unspecified acts of treason and urged the leader to expel him from both the caucus and the party. (The call to demote him was already familiar, although not in Quebec.) When Dion rejected the appeal, Chantal Hébert speculated that "only Dion's fear of a potential caucus revolt may be keeping Ignatieff in the deputy leader slot." Ignatieff, she wrote, had "commanding caucus support," and any public rebuke might bring Dion's leadership to the tipping point.[63]

In late April, Ignatieff held a fund-raising dinner for 600 guests at the Royal York Hotel that amounted to open insurrection. "His chutzpah speaks to an untested but widely held belief," reported the *National Post*. "Stéphane Dion is fated to defeat and departure. So why pretend?" Dion was absent, and his name was barely mentioned: "And then, only when Mr. Ignatieff briefly returned to formal talking points, his voice dropping an octave and plunging into unconvincing rote recitation. Perhaps this is his idea of gravitas."

Yet the most brazen spectacle was the screening of three short clips, one of which even astounded many Ignatieff supporters. The first featured Mr. Ignatieff as a 30-something journalist interviewing Pierre Trudeau shortly after the latter's withdrawal from Liberal politics. The subtext was as clear as it was powerful. The clip portrayed the two men as equals—both intellectually and as Liberals. Of all possible topics, they discussed Trudeau's rejection of socialism and embracing of the individual. This wasn't just a Liberal fundraiser, it was an unabashed snatching of the departed's great torch.

Speaker Alfred Apps introduced the next clip with a wry grin. "This is not an insurrection," he said, but "an exercise in pure nostalgia." What followed was the very Ignatieff promo clip shown on the convention floor in 2006: an uninterrupted stream of endorsements from politicians and campaign workers reminding us that Mr. Ignatieff was "the one man" who could improve Canada and take on Stephen Harper. Audacious, deliberate and engaging, it stopped short of calling for Mr. Dion's resignation. When the video started, Dion loyalists and former competitors' apparatchiks whipped out their BlackBerrys and started furiously texting in mute protest.

To corroborate Mr. Apps' plea of nostalgia, the third clip showed Mr. Ignatieff's concession speech in 2006 in which he declared his support for Mr. Dion and launched into his "tous ensemble" routine....

Mr. Ignatieff's organization stuck a fork in Mr. Dion a long time ago. But on Thursday night they welcomed everyone into the kitchen to peek in the oven and confirm that the entree is cooked. If you have any doubt in your mind, consider this: at the end of the evening, they handed out a DVD to the guests. It contained one clip: Mr. Ignatieff's convention floor movie.[64]

Ignatieff reminded his audience that evening that his leadership campaign had run for eight months on funds Barack Obama was spending in one day: "Good value for money, I'd say." He boasted that he had "raised a number of ideas—carbon tax, for one, Quebec as a nation, was another. In fact, my campaign was so full of ideas that it amounted to one long demonstration of the proposition that nothing gets you into more trouble in politics than being the first to have a bright idea." This was an adoring audience, and Ignatieff could afford to be lighthearted. He had been called the establishment candidate, but "the funny thing about being the establishment candidate was that I didn't actually know anybody in the establishment." (Senator David Smith, one of those who recruited him and campaigned for him, was sitting close by and enjoying the fun.)

Establishment or not, Ignatieff identified himself with the mass of "small L Liberal Canadians" who had built the country. "My friends, we Liberals have defined the vital centre of our nation's life for most of the last century.... We may be the natural governing party, but we must always be a party of reform.... A party of reform is a party of hope, a party that says to every Canadian, come join us, together we can be more than any of us believed we could be. That is what politics is for ... to take us farther down that road towards the light that we all want to travel." [65] Obama's surge was underway across the border, and Michael Ignatieff was ready to be swept along in its soaring slipstream of words.

Bob Rae arrived in the House of Commons after a by-election victory in March, and at once injected restraint, good humour, and spontaneity into the opposition's daily attacks on the Harper government. The Liberal caucus seemed to relax a bit. Within a few weeks John Ivison reported whispers in the caucus that "Michael Ignatieff is the man who will never be king." No one wished to be quoted by name, but Ivison judged that scepticism was "more widespread than the usual bicker, brattle and back-stabbing common to all parties." It was no coincidence that disenchantment with Ignatieff coincided with Rae's arrival. "It comes down to basic political judgement and under-standing," one MP told him. "With Rae you're dealing with someone who does know politics. There is a depth to him that allows him to interact more naturally with caucus [than

Mr. Ignatieff].” Rae worked easily with the leader and caucus while Ignatieff did not. “He doesn’t come to meetings and he doesn’t engage in the lobby.... People are noticing he’s not participating. He’s a much more polarizing figure than Bob,” said another Liberal MP. On the other hand, a senior member of “the still-active Ignatieff camp” denied any hints of discontent with the deputy leader. Despite the denial, Ivison concluded, “the impression remains that, while Mr. Ignatieff professes loyalty to Mr. Dion, he has trouble hiding his ambition. It may be that it has o’er leapt itself and his best chance to be king is already behind him.”[66]

The Liberal Party stumbled through the spring session of Parliament “locked in a cycle of bravado and timidity, eternally eager to force an election soon but forever unwilling to face one now.”[67] Paul Wells reported the anonymous views of a senior Liberal advisor in April: “You’ll hear people around Dion saying the party’s not ready for an election.... And that was probably true last fall or last spring. But today it’s horses--t. The party’s ready, more or less. Now when they say the party’s not ready, it’s code. What they mean is that the leader’s not ready. And they can’t bring themselves to tell him.”[68] Little remained in Dion’s quiver beyond his own sense of dignity, the caucus’s hesitation to confront him, and his fervent promise to produce an environmental policy that would shame the government and win the next election. The leader’s stubborn confidence in himself kept the world at bay.

Focus group testing of a tax-shifting “green” plan took place in April and May, and the party’s pollster, Michael Marzolini, warned Dion in April that the scheme was a “vote loser, not a vote winner.” Dion ignored the warning. In a second memo, during the autumn election campaign,

Marzolini wrote that "every potential argument in favour....
is comparatively weak, vague and ineffectual, when
compared to expected attacks from the Tories—which are
effective, sticky and have traction ... [T]he policy is complex,
confusing and cannot be adequately explained or defended
in one sentence, much less a 10-second clip." Dion was
advised to simplify the plan, to place it within a larger environmental framework, and to emphasize other parts of the
party program in an election campaign.[69]

Despite these concerns, in mid-June Dion made his
announcement of the Liberal "Green Shift," which called
for substantial cuts in personal and business income taxes, to
be offset over four years by new "carbon taxes" on oil, diesel,
and other carbon-emitting fuels. This was a direct challenge
to the environmental complacency of the Harper government. The plan called for various exceptions, exemptions,
and incentives, including an initial exclusion of new taxes on
car, truck, and bus fuels. The party promised "green tax"
income of up to $15.5 billion by the fourth year, to be
balanced by tax savings and new social spending that would,
theoretically, make the whole program tax neutral.[70] Dion
made clear that the "Green Shift" would be the central
element in his party's election platform—whatever doubts
other members of the party might feel. Short of deposing
him in a messy coup before an election, his MPs had no
option but to run with it: the Green Shift would either be
his making or his last hurrah. Harper immediately
denounced the plan as a crazy tax grab that would devastate
the economy, and the party was never able to offer a clear
and simple explanation of why that wasn't the case. The
launching also coincided with a sudden and dramatic
increase in the worldwide price of oil, which made the tax

shift even less attractive to Canadian consumers.

The Liberal leader—in an effort to recover face after months of abstentions in the House—began to talk about bringing down the Conservative government during the fall session. Others in the caucus thought the time was overdue, despite continuing scepticism about the leader and his green policy. But the return of Liberal nerve had come too late. Stephen Harper was already hinting that he had seen enough of a dysfunctional Parliament.

CHAPTER 7

Takeover

When Stephen Harper dissolved Parliament in September 2008 Canadians were preoccupied with the political scene across the border. The prospect of an Obama presidency looked far more attractive than anything on offer in Canada. Only twenty-seven months had passed since the previous Conservative election victory, party standings in the opinion polls had stalled, and there was no indication of majority support for anyone. Harper's own fixed-election law called for an election in October 2009, but the prime minister preferred to ignore his commitment to four-year parliaments and choose his own election date, just as prime ministers have always done. The electorate sighed and turned away.

There were vital issues of concern for Canadians in September 2008, but politicians or the public (or both) chose to keep these in the shadows. Canada's role in the Afghan War had been removed from debate by the Liberal–Conservative agreement of March 2008; major sectors of the economy, such as forestry and the auto industry, were in crisis; climate change (while escalating) had faded from the country's short-term memory; there was a major tainted-meat scare; and a catastrophic collapse of world financial markets was about to begin.

More than most campaigns, this was an election centred on leadership. Stephen Harper aimed to maintain calm by scattering small benefits in all directions, denying any crisis as the stock markets crashed, and promising a steady hand on the tiller. (His cabinet, however, had cut 45 million dollars worth of minor arts programs, which emerged as a major issue, especially in Quebec.) Stéphane Dion promised a green revolution to a national audience that couldn't understand what he was saying. Toward the end of the race, Dion briefly called in Bob Rae and then Michael Ignatieff for assistance in the national campaign. But each of them upstaged him, and both were shunted back to their ridings. Jack Layton promised to take power as prime minister. Elizabeth May offered a fresh face for the Green Party, but she was running as a long-shot in a Nova Scotia riding. Gilles Duceppe played to his Quebec nationalist core. None of them stirred the blood. While the leaders toured relentlessly and dominated the headlines, the troops kept to the trenches.

Given the sluggish state of public opinion and the first-past-the-post electoral system, predictions pointed to an outcome similar to that of 2006. As expected, on election night Stephen Harper's Conservatives inched closer to a clear majority — but missed by twelve seats. There was only one significant change: hundreds of thousands of Liberal voters stayed home, and Stéphane Dion's Liberals lost twenty seats in the House.

Dion's Choices

On election night, Stéphane Dion conceded victory to the Conservative Party and promised that the Liberal Party would cooperate with the government: "My priority, the priority of the official Opposition, will be the economy, will be the economic storm that we see around the world, will be to protect Canadians for our savings, our homes, our jobs, our pensions. And I asked Mr. Harper to make the same commitment at this time of global economic uncertainty. We stand ready to work with all political parties to make this Parliament work." He made no mention of his own future as leader of the Liberal Party.

Michael Ignatieff, responding to a question about Dion's future on the same evening, said "I think it's indecent after a man has fought heart and soul from coast to coast to coast for the sake of a party to start calling him toast or anything like that.... That's not a dignified way to talk about a man who's fought as hard as he has for this party and fought as hard as he has for Canada for so long. I owe him respect."[71] Two days later Joe Volpe, MP called for the leader's resignation. Other MPs declined public comment, but said that Ignatieff was making telephone calls ostensibly to talk about how to improve the party's prospects, but "subtly soliciting their support without explicitly asking for it."[72]

Dion was incommunicado for six days after the election. On October 20, he told an Ottawa press conference: "I failed.... The past is the past. I wish I would have succeeded." He offered his resignation as party leader, but announced that he would remain in office until a new leader could be chosen at a convention in May 2009. Until then, he felt personally responsible for reorganizing and refinancing the party. His resignation was widely expected—although Dion himself was "shocked by the pressure to make a decision about the job he had held for under two years"—but his decision to remain for six months came as a surprise to observers.

Dion blamed his failure on the vicious Conservative advertising directed against him since 2006: "This propaganda cemented the mindset of Canadians to the point that it was the main reason why we lost. There are certainly other reasons, but this is the main reason." He saw nothing to regret in his own campaign: "I consulted a lot about my own performance," he said, "and I have been told that it has been a very good one, that I have been a good campaigner. I spoke with conviction. We had a good platform."[73] Even in defeat, Dion remained insulated from the widespread judgement that his leadership had been confusing and incompetent. At this point the party executive, or the caucus, might reasonably have invited him to step aside immediately in favour of an interim leader. It did not do so—so strong is the habit of deference to the leader in the Liberal Party.[74]

For three weeks after Stéphane Dion's retirement statement, potential candidates for the succession tested the waters. In the end McKenna and Manley, Kennedy, Brison, Dryden, Coderre, Cauchon, and Hall Findlay were out. The field came down to the two runners-up from 2006, Michael Ignatieff and Bob Rae, and one newcomer, the young New Brunswick MP Dominic LeBlanc.

When Ignatieff announced "I'm in!" to reporters at the National Press Theatre on November 13, he told them that: "Leadership is about telling a story that helps Canadians make sense of their world, a story that is true, and a story that helps them to act together with courage and determination. Leadership for me is telling that true story. It's about helping people to understand and then working with them to act." The Liberal Party, under his leadership, would "outwit and outthink this government." Liberal values "run right through me: compassion, toughness of mind, generosity of spirit, fierce patriotism for the land I love. When we have faith in our values, when we listen to our fellow citizens, when we practice the politics of respect and civility, we Liberals never lose."

The press gallery was familiar with his heart-on-sleeve homilies—and sceptical. Why would he win this time? Wasn't the campaign going to be a repetition of the last one? No! No! This one was all about change, and ideas, and innovation, and all those Obama things—but of course "there is only one Obama." (Just as there was only one Mike Pearson and one Pierre Trudeau. He did not compare himself....) John Ivison remarked on "that pained, indulgent smile" from "a man who is egalitarian enough to talk down to anyone." But he conceded that Ignatieff was "persuasive enough to also suggest that Mr. Harper will have a hard time claiming [he] is not a leader.... Mr. Ignatieff has learned the hard way that the range of thought and emotion available to a prospective leader is extremely limited. You get penalized for speaking frankly, with the result that the shiny, new Ignatieff is now fluent in the bromides of politics."[75]

The *Globe and Mail* agreed that Ignatieff had matured as a politician. "But the Liberals should not get carried away just yet: Mr. Ignatieff has too much to prove to merit a coronation." Ignatieff's "somewhat ruthless takeover of much of his party's organization" had shown a certain capacity to attract "organizers and backroom veterans." But he had not yet proven that he could avoid rash judgements. Bob Rae, the editors concluded, "should be able to put Mr. Ignatieff to the test. Otherwise, they will still be getting a comparatively unknown commodity." That kind of conditional approval was common in the reviews: "What will be doubted in these trying economic times," wrote Jeffrey Simpson, "is his grasp of economics, or rather the public's perception of his grasp of economics." Ignatieff could certainly tell a story, wrote Susan Riley, but the Liberal Party "—indebted, sclerotic, top-heavy and disunited—needs a plumber above all. That would seem to call for someone with a wrench, not a narrative. We'll see."[76]

Alone among the candidates, Ignatieff had taken care since 2006 to maintain and nourish his skeleton organization in anticipation of the next campaign. It was ready for action in November 2008. His team of bright young advisors, mostly products of the Ivy League, LSE, and Oxford, appeared at his side. There were daily reports of new recruits from among the supporters of other candidates to the Ignatieff team, and a regularly updated delegate count appeared on the candidate's leadership website. From the start, Ignatieff had the support of forty of the caucus's seventy-seven members, twenty-nine former Liberal candidates, and almost fifty constituency association presidents. The campaign was being organized as efficiently as Paul Martin's run for the leadership in 2003. Bob Rae's campaign was slower to move, while Dominic LeBlanc's was hardly out of the starting gate. But as destiny would have it, whatever preparations Ignatieff's two competitors had made would count for nothing.

Parliament reassembled in mid-November with assurances from all sides of the House of Commons that civility had returned to Ottawa. The prime minister was smiling and John Baird was, for the first time in his political career, speaking softly. Everyone promised to work cooperatively to meet the economic crisis. Stephen Harper, attending emergency international meetings on the economic collapse, promised to do Canada's share by committing billions of dollars in public funds to economic stimulus. Then Finance Minister Jim Flaherty presented his economic update and unleashed chaos.

Flaherty's statement suggested that, despite the economic crisis, the government would end the fiscal year in surplus. He proposed no major economic stimuli, but introduced a range of austerity measures to demonstrate Conservative financial prudence: a freeze on public sector salaries, a two-year ban on public sector strikes, an end to existing pay equity procedures, the elimination of the vote subsidy for federal political parties, and changes to the equalization formula.[77] The statement seemed to contradict the prime minister's promise of stimulus spending made only days before; but what shocked opposition and government MPs alike was its gratuitously punitive tone. There had been no warning of the austerity measures. The proposed cancellation of the vote subsidy for political parties, in particular, would devastate the finances of the Liberals, the New Democrats, the Bloc Québécois, and the Greens. (The Conservatives, who would lose most in dollar terms, depend least on the subsidy because they run a highly successful private fund-raising operation.)

The message was quickly absorbed. The opposition's anger was genuine. The minority Conservative government seemed intent on crippling its opponents as it ignored the economic crisis. Jack Layton sought the advice of Ed Broadbent, who called Jean Chrétien; and by late evening all three opposition parties were discussing plans to defeat the minority government. That would mean either another election only three months after the last one, or a coalition government somehow cobbled together from the existing

House. Two motions of confidence arising from the financial update were scheduled for four days later, on December 1. The lights stayed on late on Parliament Hill.[78] Ambition for power, always latent on the Hill, was nakedly stalking the corridors—ambition to retain power, or to seize it.

Stephen Harper belatedly recognized the massive blunder, and made his first efforts to recover the initiative. The next day he arbitrarily postponed the confidence votes by a week, to December 8. That bought time. On the weekend, as coalition talks gelled, John Baird announced cancellation of the scheme to end vote subsidies, and Jim Flaherty announced cancellation of the ban on public sector strikes. The budget, originally planned for February, would be brought down one month early, in late January.

But the opposition could not be appeased. Trust was gone. As Canadians wondered who might lead a new government, political insiders—including both Stéphane Dion and Jack Layton—met to draft the terms of an opposition accord. None of the Liberal leadership candidates took part, although they were "kept informed." By Sunday afternoon the parties had a tentative agreement to create a Liberal–NDP coalition cabinet with a two-and-a-half year life, to consist of twenty-four members, one quarter of whom would be NDPers. The Bloc promised not to oppose the coalition on matters of confidence for eighteen months.

But there were real disagreements within the Liberal Party, among the rival leadership camps. "A senior Liberal source" told John Ivison that "the preferred option for most Liberals" was that Michael Ignatieff should become interim party leader and prime minister of a coalition government. "It is understood that Mr. Ignatieff was reluctant to sign on unless he was named interim leader. Prior to the deal being struck, sources close to Mr. Ignatieff said he was unlikely to support the deal because of concerns that a coalition government led by Mr. Dion would be a 'poisoned chalice' for the next leader." Bob Rae, on the other hand, preferred to respect the Dion–Layton deal to make Dion prime minister, and to maintain "the legitimate leadership process" to replace Dion in May. The three candidates met on Sunday night, November 30, at Ignatieff's Toronto apartment to work out a common front. "Rae is proving to be a roadblock," said the "senior Liberal source." Both options were politically risky: Dion had been rejected by the electorate, but Ignatieff had not been selected. The outcome of the meeting was agreement on Rae's approach. A Liberal caucus meeting the next day confirmed support for Dion as coalition leader; and afterwards, Ignatieff, LeBlanc, and Rae appeared together to confirm the decision. "There's no turning back," Rae told reporters. Ignatieff offered his enigmatic smile.[79]

The prime minister's line of attack was clear: the coalition was undemocratic. "Stéphane Dion," he insisted, "does not have the right to take power without an election. Canada's government should be decided by Canadians, not backroom deals. It should be your choice, not theirs."[80] (This populist appeal had resonance, although it was based on a misconception of parliamentary government.) But when the House met that day, Stephen Harper appeared dispirited, apparently ready to cede power to his adversaries. Neither his concessions nor his procedural delay were working. Writing that morning in the *Toronto Star*, Chantal Hébert had already charted his escape: "If all else fails this week, Harper will still have one last desperate cartridge left and it is the option of proroguing Parliament until January when he would come back with a full-fledged economic plan." That would "have the merit of allowing the political temperature to drop back to more normal levels."[81]

Meanwhile the execution tumbrils rolled on. In late afternoon Dion, Layton, and Duceppe appeared together at a signing ceremony that confirmed their alliance to defeat the government.[82]

As they briefly strutted the stage, other forces were at work. Stephen Harper had decided to resist; and "senior Ignatieff insiders" told reporters that "the shocking Dion coalition bid" was a disaster, a "separatist coalition." Ray Heard reported on the *Bourque Newswatch* website that an Ignatieff advisor had confided to him that "Michael is in a tenuous situation and he is feeling a lot of heat from caucus colleagues and constituents alike. Frankly, we think we got snookered by Bob Rae on this one."[83]

The surreal drama played itself out. Harper denounced the coalition in an unusual televised address to the nation, and Dion responded with an out-of-focus amateur video performance leaving viewers gasping in stunned disbelief. Next morning, Harper visited the Governor-General , who had been called back from a state visit to the Czech Republic, and emerged after more than two hours to tell the country that Parliament had been prorogued until January 26, 2009. Until then, the government could not be defeated.

Ignatieff's Choices

While the government drew breath and reorganized for a defensive budget in January, the Liberal Party began the act of regicide postponed from October. A special caucus meeting after prorogation left the issue of Dion's resignation unresolved. "What the party is discussing," Michael Ignatieff commented, "is whether there are ways in which the leadership race can be accelerated in such a way that we can present clear alternatives to the country because Mr. Dion, as everybody knows, has already announced his resignation." Ignatieff said he was not involved in these discussions. In a *Globe and Mail* essay two days later, John Manley urged his party to replace Stéphane Dion as leader before Christmas. Bob Rae and Michael Ignatieff, appearing separately on CTV's Question Period on December 7, called on Dion to step aside so that the party could choose a new leader before the resumption of Parliament. But their conflict with one another was only thinly veiled. Rae suggested that the three candidates for leader should have "the chance to talk to the membership of the party in an accelerated way," leading to a vote of the membership before the return of Parliament in January. Ignatieff agreed that the choice of leader should be "moved up," but was vague about procedure. "I'm in the race," he said, "I don't make the rules." Clean hands.[84]

Offstage, his supporters and advisors were busy making the rules. The *Globe and Mail* reported that Ignatieff had "launched a bulldozer charge at the leadership, campaigning for the party's parliamentary caucus to elect him immediately as an interim replacement for Mr. Dion." The caucus executive—knowing that at least fifty-five of the seventy-seven Liberal MPs now supported Ignatieff—met on Sunday evening and agreed on a two-stage process: an immediate choice of Ignatieff by the caucus, to be confirmed or altered by the convention in May. Dion had, effectively, been dethroned. The procedure was recommended to the national party executive for confirmation at its meeting on December 9. But Bob Rae resisted. "Speaking in Toronto, he said it is up to the party membership to decide who becomes the next leader and suggested an interim leader would have an unfair advantage in the race. The former NDP premier of Ontario added that he prefers democratic contests to coronations." He proposed a telephone and online ballot of all party members to be held in January.[85] But the bulldozer was in motion. The national executive held a special telephone consultation that evening.

On December 8, Stéphane Dion announced his resignation.

> As the Governor-General has granted a prorogation, it is a logical time for us Liberals to assess how we can best prepare our party to carry this fight forward. There is a sense in the party, and certainly in the caucus, that given these new circumstances the new leader needs to be in place before the House resumes. I agree. I recommend this course to my party and caucus. As always, I want to do what is best for my country and my party, especially when Canadians' jobs and pensions are at risk.
>
> So, I have decided to step aside as Leader of the Liberal Party effective as soon as my successor is duly chosen.[86]

The same morning, Dominic LeBlanc announced his withdrawal from the leadership race and offered his support to Ignatieff: "Michael can bring the Liberal party together in a way no other can," he said.[87]

In deference to Rae, the national executive agreed to extend the selection process to include a telephone consultation with several hundred party officials across the country; but it was clear the game was up. Next day Rae made a gracious bow to Ignatieff and joined LeBlanc in withdrawing from the contest. Ignatieff would be "interim leader" by acclamation. The formalities were observed on December 10.[88] With the skilful aid of his team, Michael Ignatieff had chosen himself as leader of the Liberal Party.

Ignatieff's first event as leader was a press conference. Ten minutes before he entered the National Press Theatre, Kady O'Malley of *Maclean's* observed that "the Palace Guard has been quietly assembling behind the pillar to my left ... four full rows of what I assume are his most loyal and/or available at short notice supporters, the average age of which one of my colleagues just estimated to be eleven. Give or take."[89] John Ivison commented that "they do sit more comfortably than in days of yore ... the Liberal leader has been in front-line politics for three years now and has learned the language appropriate for a political leader. Indignation, self-belief and resoluteness are in; anxiety, doubt and indecision are out."[90]

Ignatieff stared down the audience in self-satisfied arrogance. He derided the prime minister for his divisiveness, his economic backwardness, and his ignorance of parliamentary government. He warned Harper that it would be a *"very very* serious mistake to engage in partisan attacks against a party leader at this moment. *I hope I make myself clear....*" He insisted that he was "prepared to vote non-confidence in this government if the government does not present a budget that is in the national interest." He admitted that the Liberal Party was weak in Quebec, the West, and rural Canada. He called the West "the beating economic heart of our country's future ... where the destiny of our country's economy will be played out." He was the new sheriff in town, "at times chippy, introspective, blunt, and given to a few flights of rhetoric, demonstrating that he remains an enigma who will take some time for voters to decode."[91]

The consensus of the commentators—though not, at least openly, of opposition MPs—was that the coalition was dead. Ignatieff repeated the mantra "the coalition if necessary, but not necessarily the coalition"; but it meant no more than that he would maintain the appearance of pressure for economic stimulus in the January budget. No one believed that Ignatieff would risk defeating the government and recreating the chaos of early December; and no one believed that Harper would invite it. Everyone agreed that something had to be done about the economic crisis. Ottawa under Harper's Conservatives had lost the capacity for coherent national policy-making; and in any case, no one knew whether stimulus would work. So the government consulted, the opposition offered its general encouragement, and everyone watched Washington for a sense of direction as Barack Obama came to power.

When the House of Commons returned on January 27, there were few surprises. The government glumly produced its vast scattershot of economic remedies, without shape or sense of direction or believable estimates; the NDP and the Bloc opposed the budget without looking at it; Michael Ignatieff insisted that he and his caucus would take a few hours to read it and make their judgement; and next morning, he pronounced the government "on probation." He opened his press conference in familiar tough guy mode, listing many of the budget's real failings—and missing others. (Some of the hidden failings would take days to emerge from the budget's depths.) But that was all bluff. The Liberal Party would support the government, in return for its pledge to report three times to the House of Commons on budget implementation. The government House leader immediately signalled acceptance of the toothless Liberal amendment.

Harper—who showed little belief in what he was doing in the budget—had survived. But Ignatieff—who needed time to rebuild the Liberal Party—had misjudged his first opportunity as leader of the opposition. There were glaring weaknesses of fairness and good sense in the budget that the government would have been forced to correct if the Liberal Party had defined them in a reasonable amendment likely to attract the votes of other parties in the House. After bullying his way into the leadership in December, Michael Ignatieff played it too safe in his first test in January. Too bad for those needlessly neglected in the Harper budget.[92]

The new Liberal leader will face more tests in the coming months. What issues might show us whether he will clearly distinguish Ignatieff Liberals from Harper Conservatives? On social policy—including criminal justice and national daycare—his task should be easy, since the party has already set out clear positions. On climate change, energy, and the environment—including measures to reduce the vast damage of unregulated development in the Alberta tar sands—the signals are uncertain. (Ignatieff has already hinted at a *laissez-faire* approach like Harper's.) On Afghanistan and the Israeli–Arab conflict, there is nothing yet to distinguish Ignatieff from the official Conservative line. On human rights and the protection of Canadian citizens abroad, Ignatieff (the defender of rights in the abstract) has kept quietly in the background. On NATO and NAFTA we have few clues. On relations with the United States and America's role in the world, Canadians have only his pro-imperial views of 1999–2005, and his confusing correction of 2007, to guide us. For a reformist agenda, these are discouraging signs.

Who is this guy? What does he want?

The way in which Michael Ignatieff became leader begins to answer these questions. As the historian Ramsay Cook wrote at the end of January 2009, "Every Liberal Leader since Laurier had notable ministerial experience and each was elected by a convention. Mr. Ignatieff can claim neither, having the distinction of being the first leader to have been defeated in convention."[93] The Liberal Party, like other Canadian political parties, elects its leaders according to a constitutional process—in this case, by delegated convention. A convention was planned for May 2009 to choose a successor to Stéphane Dion. But the process was side-stepped by technically correct but improper means. The party's constitutional provision for selection of an "interim" leader could not have been intended as a means of selecting a permanent leader. (If it had been, there would have been no need for use of the term "interim" in the constitution.) An "interim" leader, by definition, is a temporary leader filling the gap between leaders selected by delegated conventions. (This was the case, for example, when Bill Graham was chosen as interim leader of the party in 2006, following the resignation of Paul Martin. It would have been the case if anyone other than the three official candidates for the leadership had been chosen for the interim period leading to the May convention.) But there can be no doubt that the intention of Michael Ignatieff and his supporters in the party was to make him permanent leader of the party in December 2009. The "interim" label was a transparent deception: since both other candidates had withdrawn, there would be no contest unless other serious candidates were to come forward. None was likely to do so, and none would pose any threat to this "interim" leader. The party organization was now under his control.

Ignatieff's installation as leader of the party revealed an excessive ambition for power in the man and his closest advisors. The political circumstances of November and December 2008 were unusual, but they did not warrant the use of these exceptional measures. The appropriate choice would have been another MP, selected to serve until the Vancouver convention. At least two MPs, John McCallum and Ralph Goodale, were frequently mentioned in public discussion of the leadership crisis. Instead Ignatieff allowed, or encouraged, his aides to ignore the spirit of the party's constitution to achieve his goal. The *Globe and Mail* described this as "a bulldozer charge at the leadership." Others might describe it as a takeover or a coup. It was an act of disrespect for the constitution of the Liberal Party. Michael Ignatieff was ruthless in his pursuit of power. That matters.

The most worrying aspect of Michael Ignatieff's political beliefs, as they emerged in his writings after 9/11, is his willingness to accept and counsel the use of morally dubious or democratically unacceptable methods by political leaders whose goals he shares—his choice of "the lesser evil," as he put it, in his support for the governments of George W. Bush and Tony Blair in their "war on terror." In Kosovo and

Iraq, he promoted aggression conducted beyond, and in violation of, the United Nations Charter, spending little effort to weigh the consequences of launching invasions that violated international law. After 9/11, he advocated the use of preventive detention, "coercive interrogation" of prisoners, and selective assassination—at a time when these methods were being used and systematically abused by the Bush administration. These are large transgressions, well beyond the mere takeover of a democratic political party— but in those cases, after all, he was only an apologist, not a participant. Nevertheless his views indicate a certain political spirit. Michael Ignatieff is willing to counsel—and to use—means in pursuit of his goals that show disrespect for moral and constitutional limits. He lacks democratic restraint. He promotes himself as a tough guy—which may not always be a bluff. He wants power, and he isn't too worried about how it is used. Canadians within and beyond the Liberal Party should be anxious about where he might take the country if he were to become prime minister.

Ignatieff places himself squarely in the Canadian progressive, reformist tradition. But his predisposition towards the interests of the powerful belies that claim. His judgement is too often the victim of his ambition.

Does this mean that I endorse Stephen Harper or Jack Layton as alternatives to Ignatieff as prime minister? No. For Canadians, the case of Ignatieff represents a deeper dilemma. Harper offers us the same dilemma. The office of prime minister is a powerful one, with too few institutional restraints upon it. It is almost beyond the law.[94] In Canada and Britain, it is an "elective monarchy." The prize of office is tempting to individuals who sense the ominous powers that it possesses. It dominates and distorts our politics. In this centralized political universe, prime ministers and their court advisors are preoccupied with polling, marketing, news management, and symbolic acts aimed at the retention of power, often to the neglect of the public good. They possess huge resources with which they can do as they please. The leaders of opposition parties, seeking the office for themselves, mirror the assumptions about power of the prime ministers they oppose. When Michael Ignatieff tells us, repeatedly, that "I will decide," he reflects—he takes for granted—his own unilateral power in the party. The Liberal Party, he assumes, is his to command.[95]

Canada's political parties must concern themselves with constraining the power of the prime minister; and equally, they must examine how their own leaders are chosen, assessed, and constrained. The Liberal Party of Canada urgently needs such reflection and such restraint. Under the leadership of Michael Ignatieff the party is unlikely to get that self-examination. The country will suffer from that failure.[96]

References

Works by Michael Ignatieff:

Blood and Belonging: Journeys into the New Nationalism. Toronto: HarperCollins, 1994.

Isaiah Berlin: A Life. Toronto: Viking/Penguin, 1998.

The Warrior's Honor: Ethnic War and the Modern Conscience. Toronto: Viking/Penguin, 1998.

Virtual War: Kosovo and Beyond. New York: Picador, 2000.

Human Rights as Politics and Idolatry. Princeton, NJ: Princeton University Press, 2003.

Empire Lite: Nation-Building in Bosnia, Kosovo and Afghanistan. Toronto: Penguin Canada, 2003.

The Lesser Evil: Political Ethics in an Age of Terror. Toronto: Penguin Canada, 2004.

Works by Other Authors:

Bamford, James. *A Pretext for War: 9/11, Iraq, and the Abuse of America's Intelligence Agencies.* New York: Anchor Books, 2005.

Clarkson, Stephen. *The Big Red Machine: How the Liberal Party Dominates Canadian Politics.* Vancouver: UBC Press, 2005.

Diebel, Linda. *Stéphane Dion: Against the Current.* Toronto: Viking Canada, 2007.

Fisk, Robert. *The Great War for Civilisation: The Conquest of the Middle East.* London: Fourth Estate, 2005.

Gross Stein, Janice, and Lang, Eugene. *The Unexpected War: Canada in Kandahar.* Toronto: Viking Canada, 2007.

Holbrooke, Richard. *To End a War.* New York: Random House, 1998.

International Commission on Kosovo. *The Kosovo Report: Report of the Independent International Commission on Kosovo.* www.reliefweb.int/library/documents/thekosovoreport.htm.

International Development Research Centre. *Report of the International Commission on Intervention and State Sovereignty.* Ottawa: International Development Research Centre, 2001.

Kolko, Gabriel. *Anatomy of a War: Vietnam, the United States, and the Modern Historical Experience.* New York: Pantheon Books, 1985.

Mann, James. *The Rise of the Vulcans: The History of Bush's War Cabinet.* New York: Viking Penguin, 2004.

Nikiforuk, Andrew. *Tar Sands: Dirty Oil and the Future of a Continent.* Vancouver: Greystone Books, 2008.

9/11 Commission. *The 9/11 Commission Report: Final Report of the National Commission on Terrorist Attacks upon the United States.* New York: W.W. Norton & Company, 2003.

Packer, George. *The Assassins' Gate: America in Iraq.* New York: Farrar, Strauss and Geroux, 2005.

Rieff, David. *A Bed for the Night: Humanitarianism in Crisis.* New York: Simon & Schuster, 2002.

Russell, Peter H. *Two Cheers for Minority Government: The Evolution of Canadian*

Parliamentary Democracy. Toronto: Emond Montgomery Publications, 2008.

Savoie, *Donald J. Court Government and the Collapse of Accountability in Canada and the United Kingdom*. Toronto, Buffalo, London: University of Toronto Press, 2008.

Sheehan, Neil. *A Bright Shining Lie: John Paul Vann and America in Vietnam*. New York: Random House, 1988.

Toope, Stephen J. *Report of Professor Stephen J. Toope, Fact Finder to the Commission of Inquiry into the Actions of Canadian Officials in Relation to Maher Arar.* Ottawa, Ontario, 14 October 2005. www.ararcommission.ca/eng.

Notes

Preface

[1] Harper's preference for fixed parliamentary terms became law in May 2007 when parliament adopted a brief amendment to the Canada Elections Act establishing a fixed, four-year term, with an escape clause that rendered it meaningless. (*Statutes of Canada 2007*, Chapter 10, 3rd May, 2007, Bill C-16.)

[2] For Part One, I interviewed Michael Ignatieff in June 2006. I was unable to arrange an interview for Part Two, despite two requests made in December 2008.

Part One

Chapter 1

[3] *Globe and Mail*, November 28, 2005. The words appear in his *Blood and Belonging: Journeys into the New Nationalism* (henceforth *Blood*), 81.

[4] *Statement by Michael Ignatieff*, November 28, 2005. As he noted in *Blood and Belonging*, Ignatieff's ancestors were Russian, but had strong ties to Ukraine. His great-grandfather, as Russian ambassador to Constantinople, had bought land in Ukraine and was buried there. His grandfather and grandmother lived in both Ukraine and Great Russia before leaving after the revolution. (See *Blood*, 80-81, 88-94).

[5] *Blood*, 79-80.

[6] The other books are: *The Warrior's Honor: Ethnic War and the Modern Conscience* (1998); *Virtual War: Kosovo and Beyond* (2000); *Human Rights as Politics and Idolatry* (2003); *Empire Lite: Nation-Building in Bosnia, Kosovo and Afghanistan* (2003); *and The Lesser Evil: Political Ethics in an Age of Terror* (2004).

[7] *Blood*, 8–9.

[8] Ibid, 9–11.

[9] Ibid, 9.

[10] Ibid, 34.

[11] Some of that history is briefly noted in *The Warrior's Honor*, 40–43.

[12] *Blood*, 39-40.

[13] Or this could have been an early indication that Ignatieff's thoughts were moving towards the doctrine of "humanitarian intervention."

[14] *Blood*, 76.

[15] Ibid, 110.

[16] Ibid, 123.

[17] Ibid, 139.

[18] Ibid, 138–139.

[19] Ibid, 139.

[20] Ibid, 161.

[21] Ibid, 186.

[22] Ibid, 186–187.

[23] Ibid, 189.

[24] *The Warrior's Honor: Ethnic War and the Modern Conscience* (henceforth *Warrior*), 7–8.

[25] Ibid, 51.

[26] Ibid, 52.

[27] Ibid, 54. Huntington makes this assertion in his book *The Clash of Civilizations and the Remaking of World Order* (1996).

[28] *Warrior*, 59.

[29] Ibid, 64–65. Ignatieff notes that modern democratic theory only arrived at this universalism through a series of stages, until the seventeenth and eighteenth century moral language of rights finally extended to entire populations. Only now, in the last few decades, have liberal societies actually begun to live by the words of John Locke and Thomas Jefferson.

[30] Ibid, 73.

[31] Ibid, 87.

[32] Ibid, 89–90.

[33] Ibid, 94.

[34] Ibid.

[35] Ibid, 95.

[36] Ibid.

[37] Ibid, 96.

[38] Ibid, 99–100.

[39] Ibid, 100–101.

[40] Ibid, 101–102.

[41] Ibid, 102.

[42] Ibid.

[43] Ibid, 105. Ignatieff neglects to mention that in Bosnia this was exactly the outcome dictated by the Dayton peace accords. An enlarged UN protection force, including Canadians, went into the country to support the civilian government as it worked out fresh accommodations among the Bosnian, Serb, and Croat communities. While Ignatieff expected in 1998 that there would be "instant intervention and quick exit," the UN force continues its work eight years later, well out of the television spotlight.

[44] Ibid, 107.

[45] Ibid, 159.

[46] Ibid, 160.

[47] Richard Holbrooke, *To End a War*, 357.

[48] *Virtual War: Kosovo and Beyond*, 11–35.

[49] Richard Falk, "Kosovo Revisited," *The Nation*, April 10, 2000. For the terms of the proposed Agreement of February 23, 1999, signed by the Kosovars, see http://jurist.law.pitt.edu/ramb.htm. The US State Department's summary of the January 31, 1999, version of the document

(www.state.gov/www/regions/eur/fs_990301_rambouillet.html) does not mention the severe limitations that the treaty would impose on Serbian sovereignty. Ignatieff discusses Rambouillet only from the perspective of the Kosovars and the Americans, not the Serbs. He reports the opinion of the State Department spokesman James Rubin that "the real point of Rambouillet was to persuade the Europeans, especially the Italians who tended to think of the Albanians as terrorists and drug traffickers, that they were actually 'the good guys.' Rambouillet was necessary, in other words, to get the Europeans to 'stop blaming the victims' and to build the resolve at NATO to use force." The American ambassador to Macedonia, Chris Hill (who was part of the American delegation at Rambouillet), told Ignatieff that the American plan was not an ultimatum designed to fail. Hill thought Milosevic was playing for time while deploying his troops to prepare for massive expulsion of the Kosovar population. "Instead of negotiating a settlement, Milosevic went for broke, hoping that NATO would bomb, the alliance would crack and he would be left in full possession of Kosovo, having restored it to Serb hands forever." It is not clear how Hill, the State Department, or Ignatieff could know the intentions of Slobodan Milosevic (Virtual War, 48, 56).

[50] The Independent International Commission on Kosovo said this: "Facing a fundamentally duplicitous negotiating partner like Milosevic, Albright and others evidently saw the deadline/ultimatum/armed peacekeeping force tactics as the only ones that could bring about a change in Serb policy in Kosovo. It was, however, a problematic strategy. International law formally outlaws the use of threat of force in international negotiations. The inherent brinkmanship of the strategy is not an approach designed to resolve underlying problems or to make war a matter of last resort" (*The Kosovo Report*, 57).

[51] *Virtual War*, 35–36; *The Kosovo Report*, 23–30.

[52] Ibid, 39–46. The Independent International Commission on Kosovo later judged that the existence of "Operation Horseshoe" remained unproven.

[53] "Doctrine of the International Community: Speech by the UK Prime Minister Tony Blair … April 22, 1999" (www.globalpolicy.org/globaliz/politics/blair.htm).

[54] *Virtual War*, 71–73.

[55] Ibid, 76–77.

[56] The article, "Is military intervention over Kosovo justified" (*Prospect*, June 1999) is reproduced as a chapter of *Virtual War*, 71–87.

[57] *Virtual War*, 71–87.

[58] Ibid, 96.

[59] Ibid, 94.

[60] Ibid, 112.

[61] Ibid, 154–155.

[62] Ibid, 213.

[63] Ibid, 214–215.

Chapter 2

[64] *Human Rights as Politics and Idolatry* (henceforth *Human Rights*), 5.

[65] Ibid, 17.

66 Ibid, 37–48.

67 "Counting bodies in Kosovo," *New York Times*, November 21, 1999.

68 *Human Rights*, 37-39.

69 Ibid, 40.

70 Ibid.

71 Ibid, 41.

72 Ibid, 43. Since Security Council decisions make binding international law, it already possesses the power to do what Ignatieff asks, although it lacks any template for action beyond its own precedents, which are not binding. Under such a new system, the new rules, too, could not compel the Council to act. See below for further discussion of efforts to define the terms of humanitarian intervention.

73 Ibid.

74 Ibid, 44.

75 Ibid, 46. This admission that NATO "unleashed" the expulsion is an advance from Ignatieff's position during the war, when he insisted that the blame lay entirely with Milosevic.

76 Ibid.

77 Ibid, 47.

78 Ibid, 47–48.

79 Ibid, 173. While the commission worked, the American election campaign of 2000 was underway. In a *New York Times* essay, Ignatieff urged the candidates to accept the need for American military intervention when cases of genocide occur: "Values trump interests. When innocent civilians are dying, America may have to intervene even when its vital interests are not at stake. But values should also hold back America from intervening too often. Americans value other people's right to govern themselves, even when they do it badly. That rules out an American imperialism, even one justified in the name of human rights." But "the only sure way to stop genocide is to deploy ground forces by sea and air … to evacuate civilians or throw defensible cordons around them, safeguarding them from attack" (*New York Times*, February 13, 2000). Three years later he advocated an imperial American invasion of Iraq. (See below).

80 Independent International Commission on Kosovo, *The Kosovo Report* (www.reliefweb.int/library/documents/thekosovoreport.htm). The commissioners met five times in Stockholm, New York, Budapest, Florence, and Johannesburg during 1999–2000, and conducted extensive interviews and seminars. Among interested parties, only the United States and Yugoslavia refused to cooperate with the commission: the United States on the ground that the commission would not limit its inquiries only to "human rights abuses perpetrated by the Federal Republic of Yugoslavia during the conflict"; Yugoslavia because it alleged that Justice Goldstone held an anti–Serb bias demonstrated when acting as chief prosecutor for the International Criminal Tribunal for the Former Yugoslavia, and because "they were opposed to commissions in principle" (*The Kosovo Report*, 8).

81 Ibid, 1. The relation between the bombing and the expulsions is treated more fully in the main text of the *Report*: "The second related issue is the

allegation that the NATO bombing campaign in fact provoked this FRY (Federal Republic of Yugoslavia) campaign, and that NATO consequently created a humanitarian disaster instead of stopping it. The latter allegation is difficult to assess. We cannot know what would have happened if NATO had not started the bombing. It is however certainly not true that NATO provoked the attacks on the civilian Kosovar population—the responsibility for that campaign rests entirely on the Belgrade government. It is nonetheless likely that the bombing campaign and the removal of the unarmed monitors created an internal environment that made such an operation feasible. The FRY forces could not hit NATO, but they could hit the Albanians who had asked for NATO's support and intervention. It was thus both revenge on the Albanians and a deliberate strategy at the same time" (*The Kosovo Report*, 31).

[82] Ibid, 2.

[83] Ibid.

[84] Ibid, 2–3.

[85] Ignatieff noted that he was the author of the commission's proposal for Kosovo's "conditional independence" (interview with Michael Igantieff, June 21, 2006).

[86] *The Kosovo Report*. 4–5, 69–71.

[87] "Axworthy launches international commission on intervention and state sovereignty," September 14, 2000, No. 233, *The Responsibility to Protect*, www.dfait–maeci.gc.ca. The commission was funded by the governments of Canada, the United Kingdom, and Switzerland, and the Carnegie, MacArthur, Rockefeller, Hewlett, and Simons Foundations.

[88] *The Responsibility to Protect*, www.responsibilitytoprotect.org (henceforth *Responsibility*).

[89] Ibid, 1.35, 2.4.

[90] Ibid, 2.4.

[91] Ibid, 8.24–8.30. These principles were explained in the body of the report, which dealt in detail with all phases of potential crises that could lead to demands for intervention and subsequent repair, recovery, and international protection.

[92] *Responsibility*, Synopsis, XI, XII.

[93] Ibid, XI–XIII.

[94] Ibid, XIII.

[95] United Nations General Assembly, "Resolution adopted by the General Assembly, 2005 World Summit Outcome", 139.

[96] "Statement by Ambassador Allan Rock … on the Draft Outcome Document for the 2005 World Summit," Permanent Mission of Canada to the United Nations, September 13, 2005. David Rieff commented on *The Responsibility to Protect* that "there is absolutely no reason to expect any other fate for such reports than that they will be ignored by the great powers whose consent and support is needed to set in motion the reforms that almost everyone agrees the international system desperately needs" (David Rieff, *A Bed for the Night: Humanitarianism in Crisis*, 18).

[97] "About the Carr Center," "Project on the Means of Intervention," "Program Areas," The Carr Center for Human Rights Policy, Harvard

University (www.ksg.harvard.edu/cchrp/about.shtml); interview with Michael Ignatieff, June 21, 2006.

[98] In the administration, the leading neoconservatives were Vice President Dick Cheney, his staff members I. Lewis "Scooter" Libby, John Hannah, and William J. Luti; in the National Security Council, Stephen Hadley, Elliott Abrams, and Zalmay Khalilzad; in the State Department, John Bolton; in the Defense Department, Paul Wolfowitz, Douglas Feith, David Wurmser, and Stephen Cambone; and on the Defense Policy Board, Richard Perle, Kenneth Adelman, and R. James Woolsey. In the media, the leaders were William Kristol, Robert Kagan, George Will, Charles Krauthammer, and others. (See James Mann, *Rise of the Vulcans: The History of Bush's War Cabinet, passim*, and George Packer, *The Assassin's Gate*, 8–65).

[99] *Empire Lite: Nation–Building in Bosnia, Kosovo and Afghanistan* (henceforth *Empire*), vii.

[100] "Bush's First Strike," *New York Times*, March 29, 2001. The newspaper sources referred to by Ignatieff were the *Jerusalem Post* and the *Sunday Telegraph*.

[101] Ibid. Writing in *Empire Lite* two years later, Ignatieff commented about the UN viceroy in Kosovo, Bernard Kouchner, that "his critics often remark, half wistfully, that what the place needs is not a veteran of the human rights movement but a General MacArthur, who rebuilt Japan and implanted a kind of democracy there after 1945." The image of MacArthur recurred in Ignatieff's conversations in these days (*Empire*, 72).

[102] "It's War—But It Doesn't Have to Be Dirty," *Guardian*, October 1, 2001.

[103] Ibid.

[104] When the Spanish government of Prime Minister Felipe Gonzalez created its own murder squads to confront the Basque separatist group ETA, it could not acknowledge this publicly because it was engaging in criminal activity matching that of the terrorists. Senior officials, but not the prime minister, were eventually charged and convicted for these activities.

[105] Mary Midgley, "Understanding the 'War on Terrorism'," *Open Democracy*, October 25, 2002 (www.openDemocracy.net).

[106] Ibid.

[107] Andrew Potter, "Choose a Side, Mr. Ignatieff," *Maclean's*, April 25, 2006.

[108] "Barbarians at the Gates," *New York Times*, February 17, 2002; "Barbarians at the Gate?", *New York Review of Books*, February 28, 2002. The differing political positions of the *Times* and the *NYRB* may have been subtly reflected in the question mark that ended the *NYRB*'s title to Ignatieff's piece.

[109] "Barbarians at the Gate?", loc. cit.

[110] Ibid.

[111] "Is the Human Rights Era Ending?" *New York Times*, February 5, 2002.

[112] Danny Postel, "From Tragedy and Bloodshed, Michael Ignatieff Draws Human–Rights Ideals," *The Chronicle of Higher Education*, March 8, 2002. But three months later, Ignatieff seemed to say the opposite: "Americans were bystanders" in the post–Second World War growth of the human rights movement. "American reticence about human rights must be emphasized," he wrote, "because it is so often argued that the modern ascendancy of human rights is inseparable from the rise of American global hegemony"

("The Rights Stuff," *New York Review of Books*, June 13, 2002).

[113] Postel, loc. cit.

[114] Ibid.

[115] "Nation-Building Lite," *New York Times Magazine*, July 28, 2002.

[116] Ibid.

[117] Ibid.

[118] Ibid.

[119] "Humanitarianism, the Human Rights Movement, and U.S. Foreign Policy: Conversation with David Rieff," *Conversations with History; Institute of International Studies, UC Berkeley*, March 11, 2003 (www.globetrotter.berkeley.edu/people3/Rieff/rieff-conO.html). Rieff is the son of Susan Sontag.

[120] Ibid.

[121] David Rieff, *A Bed for the Night: Humanitarianism in Crisis*, 13. See also pages 10–15, 71–73, 95–97.

[122] "Mission Possible?", *New York Review of Books*, December 19, 2002.

[123] *Empire*, 110–111.

[124] Ibid, 112–113.

[125] Ibid, 113.

[126] Ibid, 116.

[127] Ibid, 116–117.

[128] Ibid, 118.

[129] Ibid, 119.

[130] Ibid,, 122.

[131] Ibid, 123.

[132] Ibid, 126.

[133] Ibid, 126.

[134] Ibid, 127.

[135] Ibid, 126.

Chapter 3

[136] The minutes of "Iraq: Prime Minister's Meeting, 23 July," popularly labelled "The Downing Street memo," are quoted in the *Sunday Times*, May 1, 2005. The memo also appears in "The Downing Street Memo(s)," www.downingstreetmemo.com/memos.html.

[137] See, for example, Jack Straw to Tony Blair, Secret and Personal, PM/02/19, 25 March 2002, *Daily Telegraph*, September 18, 2004 (www.downingstreet-memo.com/strawtext.html); "Iraq: Conditions for Military Action (A Note by Officials)", July 23, 2002, (www.downingstreetmemo.com/cabinetoffice-text.html); "Special Report: The Road to War: The Crawford Deal: Did Blair Sign," *Independent on Sunday*, February 27, 2005.

[138] "President Bush Delivers Graduation Speech at West Point," June 1, 2002 (www.whitehouse.gov/news/releases/2002/06/20020601–3.html); "Bush Developing Military Policy of Striking First," *Washington Post*, June 10, 2002; National Security Council, United States National Security Strategy, September 17, 2002 (www.whitehouse.gov/nscall.html).

[139] "Blair: We Have the Evidence," *Guardian*, September 24, 2002; Iraq's Weapons of Mass Destruction: The Assessment of the British Government,

September 24, 2002
(http://news.bbc.co.uk/hol/shared/spl/hi/middle_east/02/uk_dossier_on_iraq/
html/full_dossier.stm); George Packer, The Assassins' Gate, 62.

[140] "Joint Resolution to Authorize the Use of United States Armed Forces Against Iraq," October 2, 2002
(www.whitehouse.gov/news/releases/2002/10/20021002–2.html).

[141] See, for example, "Evidence on Iraq Challenged," *Washington Post*, September 19, 2002. (The report was relegated to page A18).

[142] "Plans for the Peace to Come," *Guardian Weekly*, October 25, 2001.

[143] Ignatieff expanded on this theme in April 2002 in an article in the *Guardian*: "The time for endless negotiation between the parties is past: it is time to say that all but those settlements right on the 1967 green line must go; that the right of return is incompatible with peace and security in the region and the right must be extinguished with a cash settlement; that the UN, with funding from Europe, will establish a transitional administration to help the Palestinian state back on its feet and then prepare the ground for new elections before exiting; and, most of all, the US must then commit its own troops, and those of willing allies, not to police a ceasefire, but to enforce the solution that provides security for both populations" (*Guardian*, April 19, 2002). With its eyes firmly fixed on Baghdad, Washington was not likely to turn to the Palestinian question at that moment, which made Ignatieff's demands an odd diversion of attention.

[144] Interview with Michael Ignatieff, June 21, 2006.

[145] Interview with Michael Ignatieff, June 21, 2006; George Packer, *The Assassins' Gate*, 96–97. Makiya was a convincing source: George Packer also acknowledged that Makiya was the chief source of his own initial approval of the attack on Iraq.

[146] George Packer, "The Liberal Quandary Over Iraq," *New York Times*, December 8, 2002.

[147] "The Burden," *New York Times* Magazine, January 5, 2003. A version of the article also appeared under the title "Empire Lite" in *Prospect* magazine, February, 2003.

[148] This outburst seemed out of place. Ignatieff said later that his "rage" at the American left's opposition to the war may have helped to "push me too far" in its favour. (Interview with Michael Ignatieff, June 21, 2006).

[149] George Packer, *The Assassins' Gate*, 62.

[150] "U.S. Secretary of State Colin Powell Addresses the U.N. Security Council," February 5, 2003
(www.whitehouse.gov/news/releases/2003/02/20030205–1.html). Eventually reporters were able to discount every one of Powell's assertions about the state of the Iraqi arsenals.

[151] "Full text: Tony Blair's speech," *Guardian*, March 18, 2003.

[152] "The Way We Live Now: 3–23–03; I am Iraq," *New York Times*, March 23, 2003; "Friends disunited," *Guardian*, March 24, 2003.

[153] This passage appeared only in the *Guardian* version.

[154] The *Guardian* version, which reads: "… what risks are worth running, when our safety depends on the answer, and when the freedom of 25 million people hangs in the balance" is more confusing. Are these 25 million Iraqis? Are they

going to be threatened again? Or are they others unknown, who might have to be sacrificed for "our safety" or our safety for theirs? The puzzle is insoluble.

155 "Why Are We in Iraq? (And Liberia? And Afghanistan?)," *New York Times Magazine*, September 7, 2003.

156 Two years later, the attempt to reform the membership of the UN Security Council failed, while a bland resolution on the "responsibility to protect" was adopted by the General Assembly.

157 "The Year of Living Dangerously," *New York Times*, March 14, 2004.

158 "Lesser Evils," *New York Times Magazine*, May 2, 2004.

159 See Howard Friel and Richard Falk, *The Record of the Paper: How the* New York Times *Misrepresents U.S. Foreign Policy*; "*Excerpt: The Record of the Paper*," November 12, 2004 (www.mediabistro.com).

160 "Lesser Evils," loc. cit.

161 The Phoenix Program was established by the US in South Vietnam in 1967 "to kill, jail or intimidate into surrender the members of the secret Communist–led government the guerrillas had established in the rural areas of the South." The CIA director William Colby said in 1971 that 28,000 persons had been captured and 20,000 killed by the CIA's assassination squads, known as Provincial Reconnaissance Units, under the program. (See Neil Sheehan, *A Bright Shining Lie: John Paul Vann and America in Vietnam*, 18, 732–733; Gabriel Kolko, *Anatomy of a War: Vietnam, the United States, and the Modern Historical Experience*, 330).

162 The case with the highest profile in Canada (although not the only one) is that of Maher Arar, a Canadian computer engineer of Syrian birth, who was detained by US authorities in the autumn of 2002 and secretly rendered to Syria, where he was detained for a year and tortured before being released in October 2003. In February 2004, the Canadian government established the Commission of Inquiry into the Actions of Canadian Officials in Relation to Maher Arar (www.ararcommission.ca/eng/), which held hearings during 2004 and 2005. In October 2005, the Fact Finder appointed by the commission, Professor Stephen J. Toope, reported that Arar had suffered torture while in detention in Syria. The commission was due to report in the early spring of 2006, but the report was delayed until the autumn because of disputes between the Inquiry and the Canadian government over the release of secu-rity–related materials. The issues in dispute are the subject of hearings before the Federal Court of Canada.

163 *The Lesser Evil*, 136–137.

164 Ibid, 143.

165 Ibid, 139.

166 See, for example, the discussion of secrecy and deception in the Pentagon's Office of Special Plans in George Packer's *The Assassins' Gate*, 104–110.

167 See *The Lesser Evil*, 145–155.

168 Ibid, 155–162.

169 Ibid, 170.

170 Ronald Steel, " 'The Lesser Evil': Fight Fire with Fire," *New York Times*, July 25, 2004.

171 Friel and Falk, "Excerpt: The Record of the Paper," loc. cit.

172 Ronald Steel, " 'The Lesser Evil': Fight Fire with Fire," loc. cit. Ignatieff

replied to Steel in a letter to the Times, calling the review "a travesty." He accused Steel of trying to invent his intentions and getting them "dead wrong." "The book," Ignatieff asserted, "is designed to make people think about hard choices—like interrogation, assassination and pre-emptive war—and to show how democratic societies can make these choices without sacrificing key liberties and key constitutional restraints" (*New York Times*, August 15, 2004). Steel had not referred directly to Ignatieff's intentions, but had said "Michael Ignatieff tells us how …" which could refer to the effect of Ignatieff's arguments, whatever his intentions may have been.

[173] Anthony Lewis, "Bush and the Lesser Evil," *New York Review of Books*, May 27, 2004.

[174] "Who Are Americans to Think That Freedom Is Theirs to Spread?" *New York Times*, June 26, 2005.

[175] Mariano Aguirre, "Exporting Democracy, Revising Torture: The Complex Missions of Michael Ignatieff" (www.opendemocracy.net/conflicts/index.jsp).

[176] Ibid.

Chapter 4

[177] "Shaping Society—50 Most Influential Canadians," *Macleans*, February 18, 2002.

[178] John Geddes, "Smart Guy, Eh?", *Macleans*, June 23, 2003 (www.macleans.ca/topstories/article.jsp?content=20030623_61383_61383).

[179] Ignatieff later said: "I think I made the mistake of assuming, because I was privy to some of the planning, … I was not in any inner loop, I did not give advice to State or Defense, but I was very aware of [the] Army War College in Carlyle, Pennsylvania that put together a very, very good decision grid of the key issues that an American occupation of Iraq would have to deal with, and it did include civil insurrection. I believed on the basis of that grid which I saw prior to the invasion that someone must be listening to the Army War College… I did not anticipate just how incompetent the Americans would be, there's no question about that. But you have to take responsibility for everything and I take responsibility for assuming they would be competent." (Interview with Michael Ignatieff, June 21, 2006).

[180] Ignatieff quoted by Geddes, loc. cit.

[181] Axworthy quoted by Geddes, loc. cit.

[182] Geddes, loc. cit.

[183] "Peace, Order and Good Government: A Foreign Policy Agenda for Canada," O.D. Skelton Memorial Lecture, Foreign Affairs Canada, March 12, 2004. Ignatieff notes that earlier versions of the paper were presented in a public lecture at Carleton University in November, 2002, and at a seminar sponsored by the Clerk of the Privy Council in June, 2003. (The briefing of officials mentioned by John Geddes may have been the same occasion as this seminar mentioned by Ignatieff).

[184] "Just Say 'No': Canadian Political Leaders Should Have the Courage to Stand Up to the U.S.," *Macleans*, December 6, 2004.

[185] Peter C. Newman, "We've Seen This Before," *Maclean's*, April 27, 2005.

[186] "Speech by Michael Ignatieff," March 3, 2005 (www.liberal.ca/news_e.aspx?id=934 and www.goodreads.ca/lectures/ignatieff). The introduction by Janice Stein appears in the Good Reads version.

[187] Conor Gearty, "Legitimising Torture—With a Little Help from Our Friends," *Index on Censorship*, Issue 1, 2005. See also Laurie Taylor, "No More Mr. Nice Guy," *Toronto Star*, August 28, 2005.

[188] Laurie Taylor, loc. cit.

[189] Diane Francis, "Michael Ignatieff," *National Post*, October 26, 2005.

[190] Julian Borger, "Intelligent Designs," *Guardian*, January 20, 2006.

[191] George Ignatieff served for three years (1966–1969) as Canadian ambassador to the United Nations and in 1984 he became Canada's disarmament ambassador under Prime Minister John Turner.

[192] Timothy Brennan, "Beyond Shame and Outrage: Michael Ignatieff and the New Intellectual Barbarism of America," *Literary Review of Canada*, June 2006.

[193] Interview with Michael Ignatieff, June 21, 2006.

[194] Jeffrey Simpson, "Mr. Ignatieff's subliminal Canadianness, *Globe and Mail*, June 3, 2006.

Part Two
Chapter 5

[1] "Is Brison the key to an Ignatieff win?" *National Post*, October 3, 2006.

[2] "Debate casts Ignatieff as front-runner," *Globe and Mail*, June 12, 2006; *Mi Community: On the Record, The Michael Ignatieff Campaign Blog*, June 10, 2006. The parliamentary vote to extend the mission by two years had taken place in May, on a motion introduced with only thirty-six hours' notice by Prime Minister Harper. After a short debate, twenty-four Liberal MPs broke ranks to support the government motion. As Janice Gross Stein and Eugene Lang point out in their book *The Unexpected War: Canada in Kandahar*, the "Liberal commitment" in Afghanistan was in fact a series of separate, short-term commitments rather than a single, open-ended one.

[3] "Canada can help stop this march to the abyss," *Globe and Mail*, August 1, 2006.

[4] "Rae criticizes Liberal rival for delay," *Toronto Star*, August 2, 2006; "A bad week for Ignatieff," *Toronto Star*, August 6, 2006.

[5] "Rae criticizes Liberal rival for delay," *Toronto Star*, August 2, 2006. See also "Ignatieff details ceasefire proposal," *Globe and Mail*, August 3, 2006. The Ignatieff campaign later gave an unedited transcript of the interview to the Canadian Press, which showed that Ignatieff had preceded his remarks with the words "Qana was a tragedy…. It was a tragedy for the Lebanese and it was unfortunately a victory for Hezbollah." But he had not complained about the reporting. "One rule I understand about this," he said, "is that you're fully responsible for your words. You're even responsible when they're quoted out of context, as I believe I was in this instance." ("Ignatieff admits gaffe on Mideast," *Toronto Star*, August 11, 2006.)

[6] "A bad week for Michael Ignatieff," *Toronto Star*, August 6, 2006.

[7] "Speaking Notes for an Address by the Hon. Bob Rae, Canada needs to find its voice again in foreign policy," Munk Centre, University of Toronto, August 10, 2006.

[8] "Comments a mistake, Ignatieff says," *Globe and Mail*, August 11, 2006.

[9] Michael Ignatieff, "Kyoto and Beyond: Options for Long-Term Reductions in Canada's Greenhouse Gas Emissions," August 21, 2006; Michael Valpy, "Being Michael Ignatieff," *Globe and Mail*, August 26, 2006.

10 "'Peacekeeping died in Rwanda': Ignatieff;" "Will he run in next election;" "If he loses, will he quit?" *Toronto Star*, August 30, 2006.

11 "Ignatieff attacked for 'gaffes'," *Toronto Star*, August 31, 2006; "Ignatieff backtracks on quitting if he loses," *Globe and Mail*, August 31, 2006.

12 "Ignatieff has little to apologize for," *National Post*, September 5, 2006.

13 "It's all about Ignatieff—but it shouldn't be," *Globe and Mail*, September 2, 2006.

14 Michael Ignatieff, *Agenda for nation building: Liberal leadership for the 21st century*, September 2006.

15 "Constitution and carbon tax key elements of bold plan," *Globe and Mail*, September 7, 2006.

16 *Agenda for nation building*, 29.

17 "Ignatieff's Folly," *Globe and Mail*, September 8, 2006.

18 "Ignatieff's risky Quebec gambit," *Toronto Star*, September 13, 2006; "Ignatieff has disqualified himself," *National Post*, September 16, 2006; "Ignatieff: Liberal saviour or sorcerer?" *Toronto Star*, September 11, 2006.

19 "Anybody but Ignatieff, Axworthy tells Liberals," *Ottawa Citizen*, October 7, 2006.

20 "Rivals attack Ignatieff over Iraq, Afghanistan," *Globe and Mail*, September 18, 2006; "Gloves off in leadership debate," *Toronto Star*, September 18, 2006.

21 "Furor costs Ignatieff key backer"; Clifford Orwin, "Mr. Ignatieff's sorry version of even-handedness," *Globe and Mail*, October 12, 2006; "Ignatieff calls Harper accusations of anti-Israeli bias a 'disgrace'"; "Ignatieff's judgement the real issue," *National Post*, October 13, 2006. (Harper, in his comments, exempted Scott Brison and Joe Volpe from his sweeping condemnation.)

22 Michael Ignatieff, "Every Canadian Matters: Fighting for Equality in Harper's Canada" (www.michaelignatieff.ca/en/about/speeches/912_every-canadian-matters-fighting-f...)

23 "Ignatieff's judgement the real issue," *National Post*, October 13, 2006.

24 "Iggy just wants to be liked (really)," *Globe and Mail*, October 23, 2006.

25 Peter C. Newman, "Changing the Liberal Catechism," *National Post*, September 23, 2006. Newman names a core group of twenty-four Ignatieff advisors with an average age of twenty-five, and five "senior advisors": David Smith, Stephen Owen, Alfred Apps, Dan Brock, and Paul Zed.

26 "Ignatieff camp's new sales pitch: He'll take Quebec," *Globe and Mail*, October 20, 2006; "Even Ignatieff supporters have mixed views over his Quebec 'nation' idea," *Canadian Press*, October 24, 2006; Andrew Coyne, "Here we go again, placating Quebec," *National Post*, October 25, 2006.

27 Jeffrey Simpson, "Mr. Ignatieff's repeated errors in judgement," *Globe and Mail*, October 28, 2006; Andrew Coyne, "Here we go again, placating Quebec," *National Post*, October 25, 2006; William Johnson, "The inherent dangers in recognizing Quebec as a nation," *Globe and Mail*, October 27, 2006; James Travers, "Ignatieff rolls the dice with Quebec gambit," *Toronto Star*, October 28, 2006; Thomas Walkom, "Ontario cringes at more constitutional talk," *Toronto Star*, October 28, 2006.

28 *Globe and Mail*, October 27, 2006.

29 "Rivals cool to Quebec 'nation' debate," *Toronto Star*, October 30, 2006.

30 Michael Ignatieff, "Being equal, as Canadians, doesn't mean being the same," *Globe and Mail*, November 9, 2006.

31 Ramsay Cook, Jan Vrana, "Bye-bye, Iggy?," *Globe and Mail*, November 10, 2006.

[32] "A Nation in Canada: PM," *National Post*, November 23, 2006; "Harper's divisive Quebec gambit," *Toronto Star*, November 23, 2006; William Johnson, "Recognizing the elephant in Confederation," *Globe and Mail*, November 23, 2006; Susan Riley, "Time for another Valium," *Ottawa Citizen*, November 29, 2006.

[33] "A man with a thirst for adventure...," *Toronto Star*, November 19, 2006.

[34] Evan Solomon, "Interview: Michael Ignatieff," CBC News Sunday, November 19, 2006, www.cbc.ca.

[35] "'I hardly believe that mine is the only judgement at issue': Ignatieff," *Hill Times*, November 20, 2006.

[36] Anne Kingston, "Michael Ignatieff has turned his high beams on us. Are we good enough for him?," *Maclean's*, November 20, 2006.

[37] Evan Solomon, loc. cit.

[38] Robin V. Sears, "The Liberals: stumbling out of a hall of mirrors," *Policy Options*, February 2007, 20.

[39] "Ignatieff's hot speech leaves many cold," *Globe and Mail*, December 2, 2006.

[40] "Canadians haven't heard the end of Michael Ignatieff," *Ottawa Citizen*, December 4, 2006. Six delegates committed to Kennedy on the first ballot, thinking his third-place position safe, voted instead for Martha Hall Findlay and inadvertently put Kennedy into fourth place. If they had maintained their commitment, the outcome might have changed dramatically on the second and subsequent ballots, when Dion rather than Kennedy would have faced the option of dropping out. While Kennedy delivered all but 10 per cent of his third ballot vote to Dion, Dion would have been unlikely to do the same for Kennedy. (See Sears, loc. cit., 23; and Linda Diebel, *Stéphane Dion: Against the Current*, 216.)

[41] "Rousing political theatre ends with Dion win," *Globe and Mail Update*, December 2, 2006.

Chapter 6

[42] Linda Diebel, op. cit., 228–232.

[43] Quoted in ibid, 235.

[44] Quoted in ibid, 236–237.

[45] Rae, however, would not become an MP until March 2008, and thus was more distant from day-to-day discussion in caucus. Ignatieff and his substantial clique among Liberal MPs were in a better position to influence the debate about election timing.

[46] John Geddes, "Dion of the Living Dead," *Maclean's*, October 1, 2007.

[47] Quoted on the Conservative blogger Stephen Taylor's website, www.stephentaylor.ca/2007/10/ignatieff-laughs-behind-dions-back, October 21, 2007. The blog contained a video of Ignatieff's reactions during Dion's speech.

[48] "Ignatieff awakens to grim reality of political betrayal," *Globe and Mail*, August 3, 2007.

[49] Michael Ignatieff, "Getting Iraq Wrong," *New York Times Magazine*, August 5, 2007.

[50] "Ignatieff's tardy regret," *Toronto Star*, August 5, 2007.

[51] Joey Slinger, "Ignatieff misses again on Iraq," *Toronto Star*, August 9, 2007.

[52] Robert Sibley, "Ignatieff's about-face," *Ottawa Citizen*, August 12, 2007.

[53] "Ignatieff's mea culpa is honourable"; Don Macpherson, "Ignatieff positioning himself for Dion's fall," *Montreal Gazette*, August 7, 2007.

[54] Neil McLaughlin and Robert O'Brien, "Most academics got Iraq right," *Ottawa Citizen*, August 17, 2007.

[55] Katha Pollitt, "Who's Sorry Now," *Nation*, August 27, 2007; David Rees, "Cormac Ignatieff's 'The Road'," *Huffington Post*, August 7, 2007

[56] "How the Iraq flip-flop could pay off," *Ottawa Citizen*, August 11, 2007.

[57] "Right wing, left wing, puffin wing," *Globe and Mail*, August 31, 2007; "Politicians now at their wit's end," *Toronto Star*, September 2, 2007. (The Conservative Party did, indeed, make use of the puffin in an attack ad in 2008, but Stephen Harper ordered the ad removed when the excrement hit the website.)

[58] CTV News, December 23, 2007.

[59] "Pull the plug, PM dares Dion," *Toronto Star*, February 28, 2008; "Un general sans armée," www.cyberpresse.ca, 27 février, 2008.

[60] Scott Brison was the only other leadership candidate to favour prolonging the mission.

[61] Independent Panel on Canada's Future Role in Afghanistan, Final Report, January 2008, 33–39.

[62] See "Full text: Government motion on Afghanistan," February 8, 2008, www.cbc.ca/news/background/afghanistan/government-motion-afghanistan.html; "Liberal Amendments to the Government Motion," Liberal Party, February 12, 2008; "Revised Conservative motion on Afghanistan," March 14, 2008, www.cbc.ca/news/background/afghanistan/revised-motion-afghanistan.html; "Conservatives, Liberals extend Afghanistan mission," *Toronto Star*, March 14, 2008. Harper announced at the NATO meeting in May 2008 that Canada's conditions had been met and formally confirmed the extension of the mission.

[63] Chantal Hébert, "No breakup yet for Dion, Ignatieff," *Toronto Star*, March 31, 2008.

[64] "Ignatieff flexing leadership muscle," *National Post*, April 26, 2008.

[65] Michael Ignatieff, "Speech to the Deputy's Dinner," April 24, 2008, www.michaelignatieff.ca/en/about/speeches/1010_speech-to-the-deputys-dinner.

[66] John Ivison, "Ignatieff rubs some Liberals wrong way," *National Post*, May 17, 2008.

[67] Paul Wells, "How Stéphane Dion Broke the Liberal Party," *Maclean's*, April 21, 2008.

[68] Ibid.

[69] "Dion ignored Green Shift warnings," *Toronto Star*, October 17, 2008.

[70] "Liberal carbon plan to offer $15.5B in tax cuts," CBC News, June 18, 2008, www.cbc.ca/story/2008/06/18/liberal-carbon-plan.html. A Toronto environmental consulting firm, Green Shift Inc., protested against the Liberal Party's use of its company name. After a few months of public spatting, the party and the company announced a legal settlement of the dispute as Parliament was dissolved for the October 2008 general election. The party continued to use the name.

Chapter 7

[71] Juliet O'Neill, "Dion vows to stay the course in spite of heavy Liberal losses," Canwest News Services, October 15, 2008, http://election.globaltv.com/topstorydetail.aspx?sectionid=223&postid=50959.

[72] Joan Bryden, "Liberal MP issues first public call for Dion to quit," Canadian Press, October 16, 2008, http://cnews.canoe.ca/CNEWS/Canada/CanadaVotes/News/2008/10/16/pdf-7105311.html.

[73] "Dion out as Liberal leader," *Toronto Star*, October 21, 2008.

[74] Dion was still carrying debt from his 2006 leadership campaign, and must have believed funds could be more easily raised while he remained as leader, rather than after his departure to the backbenches. Is it possible that he offered his immediate resignation to the party executive, on condition that the party pay off the outstanding debt—and that the executive refused? Did that prompt his stubborn decision to remain for six months as a lame duck leader? An advisor to Dion said that he preferred to stay on to assure neutrality in preparing for the succession, since the two most likely candidates for the interim leadership, John McCallum and Ralph Goodale, had been supporters of Michael Ignatieff and Bob Rae, respectively, in 2006. (See "Dion out as Liberal leader," loc. cit.)

[75] Michael Ignatieff, "Statement announcing his candidacy for the leadership of the Liberal Party," November 13, 2008,www.michaelignatieff.ca/en/blog/1993_statement-announcing-his-candidacy-for-th…; Kady O'Malley, "One for the money, two for the show—Liveblogging the official launch of Michael Ignatieff's leadership campaign," November 13, 2008, http://blog. macleans .ca/2008/11/13/one-for-the-money-two-for-the-show-liveblogging-th…; John Ivison, "Witness the new Ignatieff," *National Post*, November 14, 2008.

[76] "Seasoned, but not fully tested," *Globe and Mail*, November 14, 2008; Jeffrey Simpson, "The polarization is gone—Ignatieff is the favourite," *Globe and Mail*, November 14, 2008; Susan Riley, "At last, a narrative," *Ottawa Citizen*, November 14, 2008.

[77] "Government of Canada maintains strong and responsible economic leadership," Conservative Party of Canada, November 27, 2008, www.conservative.ca/EN/1091/107684.

[78] "Harper scrambles to retain power," *Toronto Star*; Don Martin, "Harper has no one to blame but himself," *National Post*; James Travers, "Harper gives in to political temptation," *Toronto Star*; Thomas Walkom, "Hard-right Tory ideology has put the PM in a bind," *Toronto Star*, November 29, 2008.

[79] Closely similar accounts of these events, dependent on "sources," appeared in the *National Post* and the *Toronto Star*: John Ivison, "Ignatieff would lead Liberal-NDP coalition," *National Post*, December 1, 2008; Les Whittington, Bruce Campion-Smith, Tonda McCharles, "Coalition said close," *Toronto Star*, December 1, 2008. See also a later report by the same *Star* writers, "Liberals: Dion would be PM," *Toronto Star*, December 1, 2008. The *Globe and Mail*'s lead offered essentially the same story, with more reflection on the implications of Liberal indecision: Campbell Clark and Brian Laghi, "Liberals, NDP firm up deal to topple Tories," *Globe and Mail*, December 1, 2008.

[80] "Harper scrambles to retain power," *Toronto Star*, November 29, 2008.

81 Chantal Hébert, "PM's best hope: Liberal divisions," *Toronto Star*, December 1, 2008.

82 "A Policy Accord to Address the Present Economic Crisis," December 1, 2008; "One prime minister too many," *Globe and Mail*, December 2, 2008.

83 Ray Heard, "Exclusive: Iggy rethinks coalition," *Bourque Newswatch*, December 2, 2008, www.bourque.org/notes.html. That evening, Heard updated his account with a claim from "insiders" that "at least 15 opposition members are ready to break ranks and, if necessary, sit as independents." Most of these were Liberal MPs. If they had done so, the government would not have been defeated in the confidence votes scheduled for December 8. But prorogation intervened and the prospect of a shattered Liberal caucus evaporated.

84 "Quick exit for Dion possible: Ignatieff," *Toronto Star*, December 6, 2008; John Manley, "The first Liberal step: Replace Dion," *Globe and Mail*, December 6, 2008; "Rae and Ignatieff call for Dion to step aside," *National Post Mobile*, December 7, 2008, www.nationalpost.com/most_popular/story.html?id=1044556.

85 Brian Laghi and Campbell Clark, with reports from Michael Valpy ... Daniel Leblanc, Jane Taber and Bill Curry.... and The Canadian Press, "Liberal battle lines are drawn," *Globe and Mail Update*, December 8, 2008, www.theglobeandmail.com/servlet/story/RTGAM.20081208.wPOLliberals12 08/B... Steven MacKinnon, who was Ignatieff's national campaign director and a central participant in the negotiations over the succession, held that the party constitution did not permit the process favoured by Rae. In the event of a leader's resignation, he said, an interim leader could only be chosen by the national executive in consultation with the Liberal parliamentary caucus. MacKinnon's view is misleading. Rae's proposal could have been accepted by the executive, a shortened campaign and poll could have been conducted in January, and the caucus and executive could have followed the correct constitutional procedure in ratifying it. ("LeBlanc to drop out of Liberal leadership race, support Ignatieff," CBC News, December 7, 2008, www.cbc.ca/canada/story/2008/12/07/liberals-leblanc.html?ref=rss.)

86 Laghi and Clark, loc. cit.

87 Ibid.

88 "Liberals get to work under Ignatieff," *Toronto Star*, December 10, 2008; Liberal Party of Canada, "Statement by Liberal Party President Doug Ferguson on the Selection of an Interim Leader," December 10, 2008, www.liberal.ca/story_15534_e.aspx. Ferguson said that the executive's consultations "revealed an overwhelming consensus in favour of one individual.... I am pleased to announce that the National Executive has voted unanimously to appoint Michael Ignatieff as Interim Leader of the Liberal Party of Canada."

89 Kady O'Malley, "Good King Ignatieff looked out...," *Macleans*.ca, December 10, 2008, http://blog.macleans.ca/2008/12/10/good-king-ignatieff-looked-out/print/.

90 John Ivison, "Ignatieff backs away from the cliff," *National Post*, December 11, 2008.

91 Bruce Campion-Smith, "Ignatieff flexes his muscles," *Toronto Star*, December 11, 2008.

92 There is a constitutional reason why Ignatieff needed to offer a substantial amendment to the budget motion at this time—if he really intended to put

pressure on the Harper government. In a new minority Parliament, constitutional convention suggests that there is an interim period of about six months in which the government is on trial in the House. During that time, defeat on a confidence motion means that the Governor-General would not automatically grant dissolution to the prime minister if he were to request it, but might instead invite another MP (probably the leader of the opposition) to seek the House's confidence. After that period of trial, a defeat on a confidence motion would normally justify the prime minister's request to dissolve and call an election. The trial period means that both government and opposition are uncertain of the consequences of defeat—but the government risks more than the opposition if it courts defeat because it (perhaps) lacks the option of dissolution. The opposition leader, by contrast, faces the possibility that he really might be asked to form a government. By the time Ignatieff's first probationary report comes due, however, this trial period will have passed, and the prime minister will be justified in asking for dissolution if defeated. Ignatieff would then be in a weaker position than the prime minister if he rolled the dice. Since he did not wish to take the risk of an invitation to form a coalition government, Ignatieff backed off the challenge on January 28, 2009.

[93] Ramsay Cook, "Mr. Ignatieff's real difference," Letters, *Globe and Mail*, January 31, 2009. Cook's letter was in reply to a column by Peter C. Newman, who argued that, although Ignatieff is a carpetbagger or interloper in politics, the Liberal Party was simply following its own tradition in choosing an outsider as leader. This is a remarkable case of shaping history to fit the argument. (Peter C. Newman, "Prodigal sons inherit the party's crown," *Globe and Mail*, January 30, 2009.)

[94] See especially Donald Savoie, *Court Government and the Collapse of Accountability in Canada and the United Kingdom*, and Peter H. Russell, *Two Cheers for Minority Government: The evolution of Canadian parliamentary democracy.* (My own first contribution to this debate appeared in 1969, in "President and Parliament: The Transformation of Parliamentary Government in Canada," reprinted in Schultz, Kruhlak, Terry, *The Canadian Political Process*, 1970.)

[95] Paradoxically, Michael Ignatieff needs the confirmation of a leadership convention to legitimize the power that he already claims, because that is what the party constitution requires. But that same legitimization by a national convention deprives the parliamentary caucus of any power to control him. A serious attempt to limit the party leader's power might well involve changing the party constitution so that the leader must be chosen by the caucus, or by a body in which the caucus forms the majority. Such a change would do much to restore the power of the House of Commons and of individual MPs. The historian Christopher Moore, among others, has been urging this democratic reform for many years.

[96] There were two small but encouraging signs from Ignatieff's office in February 2009. One was his agreement with six Newfoundland Liberal MPs to permit them to vote against the Harper budget without penalty, because of their objection to changes in the equalization formula. The second was his institution of daily consultation with a "kitchen cabinet" of Liberal MPs. Reformist logic might suggest that this advisory group should be chosen by election from the caucus, rather than by the leader's personal selection. As it stands, the group could be terminated at any time by the leader's fiat. (See "Ignatieff draws criticism for letting MPs break ranks," *Globe and Mail*, February 4, 2009; Lawrence Martin, "Ignatieff's kitchen cabinet signals a new way," *Globe and Mail*, February 5, 2009.)

Index